W9-AQQ-865

ETHICS

and the

ARCHIVAL

PROFESSION

Introduction and
Case Studies

Karen Benedict

CHICAGO

The Society of American Archivists
527 S. Wells Street, 5th Floor
Chicago, IL 60607-3992 USA
312/922-0140 • fax 312/347-1452
www.archivists.org

© 2003 by the Society of American Archivists. All rights reserved.
Second printing 2006
Printed in the United States of America

Library of Congress Cataloging-in-Publication Data

Benedict, Karen M.
   Ethics and the archival profession : introduction and case studies / Karen Benedict.
      p. cm.
   Includes bibliographical references.
   ISBN 1-931666-05-9 (alk. paper)
   1. Archivists—Professional ethics—Case studies. 2. Appraisal of archival materials—Case
studies. 3. Archives—Access control—Case studies. 4. Archives—Administration—Standards.
5. Archives—Law and legislation. I. Society of American Archivists. II. Title.
   CD971.B46 2003
   174'.902—dc22

                                                                              2003059223

CONTENTS

Introduction

WHAT IS PROFESSIONAL ETHICS?

Through the process of creating and adopting a code of ethics, a profession defines for itself how it expects individual members and institutions to conduct themselves in performing their professional duties. Such a code provides the members guidance in understanding their moral responsibilities and their obligations to society in a professional context.

The Society of American Archivists (SAA) developed the first code of ethics for the archival profession. Therefore it had a significant influence on the associations of other countries. Not all subsequent codes emulate the U.S. model, but their creators looked to it as a guide and resource.

It is important to understand the meaning of the terms "ethics" and "professional ethics." Ethics is a branch of moral philosophy. It deals with norms of conduct or "moral behavior"—not necessarily good behavior, but behavior that results from making a moral choice.

According to Oliver Johnson in his work *Ethics: A Source Book*, "Ethics is concerned with attempting to answer two different questions, which might be stated as follows: What is right (or wrong)? what is good (or evil)?" [1]

To answer these questions, ethicists have two different approaches: deontological and teleological. Deontologies discuss actions or duties in terms of rightness or wrongness. Teleologies deal with the good or bad results from choices that are made. In practical terms, a deontology may be prescriptive, and list appropriate actions that should be taken, or proscriptive, and list inappropriate actions that should not be taken. On the other hand, a teleology analyzes the desirable or undesirable results of particular actions. Typically, professional codes of ethics have a bit of both approaches to moral decision making.

In their work *Professional Ethics and Librarians*, Jonathan A. Lindsey and Ann E. Prentice give a brief history of the development of ethical codes in the United States. They point out that the origin of the modern code dates to the middle of the nineteenth century. The American Medical Association adopted a code of ethics in 1848 when it was organized. "Between 1890 and 1924, more than 200 American business and professional groups adopted codes of ethics. . . . During the last 75 years, nearly every profession has considered and often adopted

---

[1] From Oliver A. Johnson, *Ethics: A Source Book* (New York: Holt, Rinehart and Winston, 1958), 8.

codes of ethics." [2] The Society of American Archivists took part in that U.S. trend by creating its "Code of Ethics."

Johan Bekker, a leading authority on ethics in librarianship, offers the following motivation for creating professional ethical codes in his 1976 dissertation, *Professional Ethics and Its Application to Librarianship*. [3] Bekker finds that, "In order to gain or retain the confidence of society, a professional group develops and imposes on itself regulatory standards of behavior, usually of a higher ethical nature than dictated by law or common morality, to which they hold themselves and other members of the group responsible. The set of standards that each profession sets for itself and which it is willing to enforce is an indicator of how much responsibility it accepts for the protection of the public."

An important aspect of a professional code of ethics is its public function. In addition to guiding practitioners, the code also serves as a compact with the public. It promises that the special expertise of the group will be used in pursuit of the highest goals of the profession and for the greater good of society. An ethical code sets moral standards for the members of a profession and it establishes approved bounds within which to conduct one's work.

When creating a code of ethics, a profession must wrestle with the conflicts that arise between purely ethical concerns and the realities of the workplace and societal pressure upon the members. It is difficult to resolve these conflicts between the highest levels of professional conduct and the sometimes questionable, but typical, practices that occur in everyday work situations.

In the introduction to his book *Ethics and Professionalism*, John Kultgen begins with a series of questions that aptly define these problems. He asks:

> Is it a moral obligation to be as professional as possible in one's work? And is it a mark of professionalism to act morally? Or do professionalism and morality have nothing to do with one another?
>
> On the one hand, should one always do one's work in a professional manner or does morality sometimes demand unprofessional conduct? Must one ever violate the standards of professionalism in the name of something more important?
>
> On the other hand, must professionals remain scrupulously moral in order to adhere to the standards of professionalism? Employers and clients sometimes demand questionable actions of professionals precisely in their capacity as professionals—should they accede to such demands? What if acquiescence is necessary to remain on the job or in the profession? [4]

---

[2] Jonathan A. Lindsey and Ann E. Prentice, *Professional Ethics and Librarians* (Phoenix: Oryx Press, 1985), 6–7.

[3] Johan Bekker, *Professional Ethics and Its Application to Librarianship* (Cleveland: Case Western Reserve University, 1976), 1, 79f.

[4] John Kultgen, *Ethics and Professionalism* (Philadelphia: University of Pennsylvania Press, 1988), 3.

These questions underlie every profession's attempt to define ethical conduct, as well as every person's efforts to behave in an "ethical" manner in their professional capacity. Kultgen says:

> Some of the practices of the professions are defective from the moral point of view, despite the impression conveyed by their codes of ethics and other ideological instruments. The manifest functions of professions disguise an orientation that is inimical in some ways to the public welfare. . . . Major deficiencies in professional morality are due to the structure of the professions rather than defects of character in professionals. A profession is an institution that confronts individuals as a reality to which they must relate without the ability to change it significantly.[5]

Despite or perhaps because of these contradictions that exist between standard professional practice and morality, professional associations establish codes of ethics because their members require guidance to help them resolve the dilemmas and demands they face in their working lives. For archivists as for doctors, lawyers, journalists, teachers, and librarians, the ability to resolve moral conflicts affects the welfare of the public we serve, it affects the quality of our work life, and it determines the satisfaction we take in our careers.

As Kultgen points out, ethics involves knowledge of and adherence to the law, although obeying the law and behaving ethically are not necessarily synonymous. Actions that violate the ethical canons of a profession may not be illegal. For example, it would not be illegal for an archivist cultivating a potential donor to disparage the ability of a rival institution to adequately process, preserve, and provide access to the collection. However, according to the SAA "Code of Ethics" it is unethical to do so. Or it would not be illegal for an archivist to personally collect manuscripts or autographed letters of famous individuals whose papers are part of his or her institution's holdings, but it would be a breach of ethics for that individual to use his or her position and contacts to privately purchase or sell these materials in direct competition with that archivist's employing institution.

The conclusion can be drawn that although a code of ethics serves both an important internal function for a profession and a necessary external connection to the public served by that profession, nonetheless it is a daunting task for a profession to create a code of ethics that presents moral absolutes in an arena where there are many competing, sometimes more fundamental, practical, and pragmatic issues that must be addressed.

---

[5] Ibid., 4

Chapter One

ETHICS VERSUS PROFESSIONAL CONDUCT

In the 1990s, archivists around the world addressed the importance of ethics to the profession, and during this time, many archival associations developed their own codes of ethics.[6] Interestingly, a comparison of these codes yields a list of ten ethical principles that are accepted worldwide. The ten principles are similar to those adopted by the Society of American Archivists in its 1992 revision of its code. Simply stated, the ethical principles that have global acceptance are:

1. Archivists should treat both users and colleagues fairly, without discrimination or preference on any basis.

2. Archivists must preserve and protect the intellectual and physical integrity of the records in their custody.

3. Archivists may never alter, manipulate, or destroy data in records in their custody to conceal facts or to distort evidence.

4. Archivists should discourage restricting access to records except for essential reasons of legality, privacy, or confidentiality. Archivists must inform users of all access restrictions and apply them without preference or bias.

5. Archivists should protect the privacy of donors, users, and individuals who are the subject of records. They should respect the confidentiality of information in the records in their custody and faithfully observe all legal and legitimate restrictions on access.

6. Archivists may never personally profit from privileged information about, or access to, records in their custody.

---

[6] In 1991, the Association des Archivistes du Quebec wrote its code. In 1992, the Association of Canadian Archivists adopted a code, and SAA produced a revised version of its 1980 code. In June 1993, the Association of Australian Archivists created its code, as did the New Zealand Association of Archivists in July of that year. The United Kingdom's Society of Archivists took a different approach and developed a code of professional conduct instead of a code of ethics in 1994. Finally, in 1996 at the International Congress in Beijing, the International Council on Archives formally adopted the "International Code of Ethics" that was created by ICA's Section on Professional Associations. The ICA's code was designed to be a universally applicable, and internationally accepted, standard for ethical and professional conduct. ICA has promoted its adoption by archival associations worldwide that have not developed their own codes of ethics.

7. Archivists should use impartial judgment when appraising records. They should not allow personal beliefs or biases to affect their decisions about recordkeeping.

8. Archivists do not publicly disparage their colleagues, their employing institution, or other archival institutions. Professional redress or, if unavoidable, legal action are the appropriate methods for dispute resolution.

9. Archivists should not personally collect manuscripts, personal papers, or archival records in competition with their employing institutions; nor may they act as agents for others to do so. Neither should they appraise the fiscal value of collections of donors to their own institution or the holdings of their institution.

10. Archivists should use their specialized knowledge and expertise for the benefit of society.

This list of the basic ethical principles is clear and succinct. However, additional guidance may be necessary to help archivists and archival institutions apply these principles in daily practice and to solve any problems that may arise. SAA has tried to increase understanding through an explanatory commentary after each section of its "Code of Ethics." However, legal counsel has advised the Society that this method may present some liabilities. The commentaries in the 1992 code necessarily are limited in the number of examples they can provide, and they can be interpreted to restrict the scope of legitimate responses. A better approach may be to provide case studies separate from the code. The cases should discuss the pros and cons of various actions and their ethical implications.

Both the 1980 code and the revised 1992 code adopted by SAA include principles of professional conduct for individuals and best practices for institutions in addition to ethical principles. For example, section III of the 1992 code, Collecting Policies, says, ". . . legitimate complaints about an institution or an archivist may be made through proper channels, but giving false information to potential donors or in any way casting aspersions on other institutions or other archivists is unprofessional conduct." Section IV, Relations with Donors, and Restrictions, states, "Archivists realize that there are many projects, especially for editing and publication, that seem to require reservation for exclusive use. Archivists should discourage this practice. When it is not possible to avoid it entirely, archivists should try to limit such restrictions. . . . " Section VIII, Use and Restrictions, says, "Archivists answer courteously and with a spirit of helpfulness all reasonable inquiries about their holdings. . . . "

There is an inherent problem in not making a clear differentiation between ethics and professional conduct because an unethical act is a more serious violation than a breach of professional conduct, such as being rude or discourteous. SAA has never set formal standards for best practices for institutions, and therefore it is not wise to issue blanket statements in the "Code of Ethics" about institutional standards. Part of the difficulty is that our profession is made up of diverse types of institutions, both public and private.

Actions that may be deemed correct practice for government archives may not be best practice for private historical societies or business archives. For instance, government archives must make their records available to everyone desiring access for research purposes, but private institutions do not have that obligation and may operate solely for the benefit of their employees in business or their members in private societies. We all recognize that appropriate environmental controls are essential for long-term preservation of archival records in all formats, but in reality many institutions cannot afford to provide HVAC systems that can maintain appropriate temperature and humidity levels. We don't sanction these institutions for substandard performance, but understand that lack of resources may make it impossible for them to provide environmental controls that meet the requirements. If a repository fails to meet recognized standards of best institutional practice, then it should review its procedures, staffing levels, staff qualifications, and the allocation of resources to set priorities that will raise its performance level in the areas that need improvement.

Unprofessional conduct, although meriting reprimand and behavioral correction, primarily reflects poor professional judgment or inadequate training and experience to deal with difficult situations. On the other hand, a violation of the ethical code goes against the moral standards of the profession. It represents a serious infraction by an individual or institution. It requires that the offender take immediate action to correct or eliminate the problem.

Providing ethical principles, guidance for professional conduct, and institutional best practices are all-important activities for the Society. However, the "Code of Ethics," guidelines for professional conduct, and institutional best practices should be recognized as separate types of guidance requiring different standards for compliance. What constitutes appropriate professional conduct merits more thoughtful analysis to determine the types of conduct that are universally required and those that are institutionally specific. For the most part, acceptable standards for conduct are set by employers as a measure for reviewing job performance.

The issues of professional conduct that deserve professionwide attention involve the duties and obligations of an archivist to his or her employing institution. It is implicit in our "Code of Ethics" that archivists owe loyalty to their employers. Archivists should work to further their institutions' best interests, goals, and objectives. They should seek to enhance their institutions' good reputation and prestige in the profession.

However, there are ethical questions about how far this loyalty must go. Is there a point at which an archivist's personal morality may lead to a confrontation with the institution? For instance, what are an archivist's obligations to potential donors and users if the archivist is aware of serious deficiencies in staffing, funding, or physical facilities that put collections, and possibly users, at risk? What should an archivist do if the institution misleads donors as to the manner in which their materials will be handled? How should an archivist respond if he or she discovers that the institution has purposefully or inadvertently engaged in illegal activity?

As John Kultgen pointed out in his work, it is extremely difficult for any profession to effectively police itself. Professional ethics and personal morality are not synonymous and may, on occasion, come into conflict. The realities of the workplace dictate that professions lean toward practicality in their approach to ethics. A profession will not, and cannot, set the bar so high that it places unrealistic demands upon individual or institutional performance in a competitive market.[7]

So, the question is, should an archivist's first loyalty always be to his or her employer? What if objecting to decisions, policies, or procedures puts the archivist's job in jeopardy? Is it unprofessional, or even immoral, to choose to keep silent or to cooperate in questionable actions to maintain one's employment if there is no other viable option?

Let us look at these questions in the context of a real event. Beginning in January 1997, the *New York Times* featured articles about a guard at the Union Bank of Switzerland in Zurich who had saved archival documents that were about to be shredded. At the time, the Swiss government had ordered banks to preserve all documents relating to dealings with the Nazi government and with the deposits of Jewish clients during World War II. Charges had been made that Swiss banks had collaborated with the Nazis in protecting assets of the Nazi government, including money and property seized from Jews during the war. It also was alleged that the banks had deliberately withheld information about the existence of accounts of Jewish clients who were Holocaust victims.

In response, the Swiss Parliament passed a law to establish an independent historical commission to look into the country's financial dealing with the Nazis. It temporarily lifted bank secrecy regulations and called for imprisonment or a fine of up to $36,000 for the destruction of records.

Investigations were underway when the guard found these old records "including minute books dating back more than a hundred years and other documents relating to Jewish-held assets" in two containers clearly marked for destruction in a cellar. He took some of the material and hid it until he had time to examine it more closely, thereby preventing its destruction. The archivist for the Union Bank had not intervened to prevent the destruction of these documents despite the governmental declaration, nor had he notified authorities.

The incident made international news and Swiss feelings ran high. Just two weeks earlier, at the time of his leaving office, Swiss President

---

[7] Kultgen, *Ethics and Professionalism.*

Jean-Pascal Delamuraz had declared the American effort to create a compensation fund for Holocaust survivors "extortion and blackmail." People were angry that Switzerland's reputation for neutrality during the war was being sullied and were shocked by revelations that there appeared to have been close cooperation by the Swiss banking industry with the Nazis.

The documents that were saved had originated with the Eidgenoessische Bank, a small bank that was known to have had widespread interests in Nazi Germany. The Eidgenossische was consolidated into Union Bank at the end of the war. In July of 1997, the bank admitted that from research in its archives, the documents in question showed that the smaller bank had bought thirty-one properties in Germany, including twenty from a Swiss family and possibly three from Jews in the Berlin area in 1937. This was at the time when the Nazis forced Jews to sell land and other property. The bank had acted as intermediary in those transactions.

The guard turned over the records he had saved to a Swiss Jewish organization, which then notified the press and the government of the bank's actions. He lost his job with the security firm that employed him to guard the bank. He and his family received death threats. He eventually immigrated to the United States to escape persecution and to find employment. The bank denied that the shredding of documents was a deliberate act by responsible parties, but was fined for its actions. It has gone on to prosper and become the largest bank in Switzerland. The archivist retained his position. The sentiment of the Swiss people was against the guard for his disloyalty and for the theft of documents. [8]

Was the archivist unethical in his conduct? Was he unprofessional? What about the behavior of the guard? As in all cases involving professional ethics and conduct, the answers are complicated. A good lawyer could argue either side. It had just been declared illegal for the bank to destroy these records. The documents potentially implicated the Eidgenoissische Bank in pro-Nazi activities. However, taking the records was stealing because they were the property of the bank and not of the archivist or the guard. The events in question occurred before the Union Bank took over the Eidgenoissische, and no one from the present bank was involved. Yet these revelations would compromise the operations of the current bank. Why should the current administration bear responsibility for the actions of a different institution and people over whom it had no jurisdiction?

The evidence indicates it was not the archivist's decision to destroy records. It does not appear that he could have prevented the action by any means other than notifying the press or authorities or by acting as the guard did to take records that were not his property. If he had taken those actions, his fate probably would have been to lose his job like the guard did. He and his family

---

[8] See the *New York Times*, January 15, 1997, "Swiss Bank Shreds War-Era Data But a Suspicious Guard Halts It," by David E. Sanger; and the *New York Times*, July 29, 1997, "Latest Swiss Bank Surprise: Secrets from the Shredder," by Alan Cowell.

probably would have received similar threats. It is unlikely he could have found another archival position in Switzerland. Professionally, the archivist may not have had a choice.

On the other hand, to take no action, if he was informed, made the archivist an accessory to the illegal destruction of evidence. In terms of professional ethics, it was a choice between destroying records and participating in the cover-up of pro-Nazi activities by Swiss banks, or blowing the whistle on his employer, stealing property, and jeopardizing the jobs of other employees. In legal terms, it was an attempt by the bank to thwart efforts to restore property to the rightful owners or their heirs through illegally destroying evidence the bank had been mandated to keep. The archivist's personal ethics might have led him to act as the guard did, or at least to copy samples of the records to preserve and protect what information he could to document what had happened in the past. Alternately, he might have tried to negotiate with bank executives to halt the destruction of records on grounds that he would be compelled to reveal the bank's action when questioned by the newly appointed commission in the course of its research efforts.

In cases such as this, each archivist must evaluate his or her own options. Professional ethics may not provide an easy answer, nor protect one's course of action against legal consequences. Ultimately, each person must answer to his or her own conscience if personal and professional morality conflict.

Chapter Two

THE IMPACT OF ETHICS ON INSTITUTIONAL PRACTICES

The archival profession faces a significant challenge in setting standards for best institutional practices because so many different types of institutions exist within the profession and they have different modes of governance, missions, functions, obligations, and users. As members of a profession, we may all be bound by the same ethical principles, but acceptable conduct and practices vary according to institutional culture, law, and basic structure. For example, government archives hold public records, many of which must be maintained by law. Records that are not restricted or classified by departments or agencies are available to the public on a free and equitable basis. Governmental records are subject to the Freedom of Information Act, guaranteeing citizens' right to access to information about themselves and their activities. Privacy laws protect people during their lifetimes from public disclosure of personal information about their lives and livelihoods. The opposite is true of the records of most private institutions. The records of businesses are private. Businesses may maintain a percentage of information for financial and legal purposes, but nothing requires that other records be kept. As with personal papers, private business records needn't be made accessible to the public. Public colleges and universities are obliged to open records because they are public institutions supported by governmental funding, but private colleges and universities have no similar requirement unless they receive financial support from the government. It is not essential to list all the differences to make the point that the term "archives" encompasses a broad spectrum of institutions that do not share the same duties and obligations to their parent bodies. By extension, the archivists who serve these institutions have different functions and different obligations as well.

The profession faces a serious challenge if the goal is to provide meaningful guidance to all archives, historical societies, and manuscript repositories when they have dissimilar structure, responsibilities, and resources and they serve different constituencies. The creators of SAA's codes of ethics have recognized the need to address at least some universal issues of institutional practice, but because it is difficult to create standards for all the different categories of institutions, the compromise has been to address only a few general points.

As in the case of professional conduct, institutional practice is primarily discussed in the commentary to the 1992 "Code of Ethics." Point III deals with collecting policies. It stresses cooperation and the avoidance of competition for acquisitions. The commentary cites this as a difficult area for the profession to harmonize with ethical ideals and practice. The essential precepts are as follows:

1. It is essential to have a written collection policy.

2. Institutions must have adequate resources to deal with acquisitions.

3. The collection policy should be consistent with the mission of the archives.

4. Institutions should avoid competing for collections, particularly personal papers that should be kept together in a single repository.

Discussion revolves around the code's call for cooperation rather than competition, while at the same time acknowledging that institutions operate independently of one another and that "there will always be room for legitimate competition." Unanswered are the questions of what is legitimate competition and who should make that judgment? Is it really up to the professional association to stifle competition between or among institutions? Could that be viewed as a violation of the law? The commentary raises another problem when it goes on to say, "It is sometimes hard to determine whether competition is wasteful. Because owners are free to offer collections to several institutions, there will be duplication of effort. This kind of competition is unavoidable. Archivists cannot always avoid the increased labor and expense of such transactions."

Although this undoubtedly is an accurate assessment of the problem, it does not offer useful guidance for resolving conflicts or bad feelings that arise from such competition. Without standards and benchmarks against which to measure institutional performance, it is difficult to assess which repositories provide the best home for materials.

Neither does the current code discuss the problem of institutional records that have strayed, been stolen and placed on the market, appeared in other institutional holdings, or been lost or inadvertently thrown away. In some cases, governmental and business records may be being treated as "manuscripts" by an "inappropriate repository." Meyer Fishbein addressed this problem in the commentary to the 1980 code. Fishbein pointed out that, "Replevin by public agencies is a difficult legal process."

Additional guidelines for best institutional practice in the area of collecting policies need to be developed to offer archivists appropriate alternatives for resolving these sorts of collecting conflicts. These might include, in the case of personal papers, giving priority to an institution that already holds some of the individual's papers; requiring the return of original archival records to the creating body; or setting up third-party mediation by an uninvolved institution when there is rancorous competition between institutions for a collection.

Donor relations are another area of institutional concern. Although all archivists know the importance of creating a systematic and well-documented process for negotiating and accepting donations and deposits of material, this practice sometimes is honored in the breach—or was not a policy of earlier administrations—leaving large segments of holdings without proper documentation. Every archival institution should be scrupulous in documenting its contractual relationship with donors and depositors of material. Because donors may have unrealistic expectations about the research value of their materials; how the documents will be kept and made available for use; their rights of ownership and ability to control access; and the institution's future right to dispose of all or part of their donation, it is the institution's obligation to provide donors with clear and unequivocal information about these issues.

Donor and deposit issues comingle the institution's ethical and legal obligations. Confusion frequently seems to arise within the profession between what are *legal* and what are *ethical* obligations. Copyright, intellectual property rights, tax consequences, and privacy are matters of law. The institution's obligation is to know and to obey the law. It also is the institution's responsibility to inform donors and researchers about pertinent laws to facilitate their compliance.

The ethical obligations of institutions include

1. Providing access to materials;

2. Respecting confidentiality and sensitivity of information that does not fall under privacy law; and

3. Protecting and preserving the authenticity of the documents in its collections.

The ethical code clearly states that institutions should discourage donors from imposing conditions on gifts or restricting access to collections except for restrictions required by law to protect the privacy of individuals whose rights would be compromised by free disclosure.

The regulations of the Internal Revenue Service prohibit any member of an institution's staff from appraising donations to the institution for tax purposes.

As an institution negotiates donor or deposit agreements, or later when processing materials, it may discover that some documents contain information that can be construed as confidential or sensitive where discretion, but not law, leads the institution to consider restricting access for a period of time. In other cases, the potential donor may want to control access to the material during his or her lifetime. It is important to remember when you choose to exceed legal requirements that you are making a personal judgment that information is scandalous or derogatory, or it has potential to cause emotional pain to individuals. This is a gray area where institutions need to carefully weigh and balance their ethical obligations in light of their institutional mission and duty to the users they serve. It is important for the institution to have a written and well-defined acquisition and collection policy statement that enables staff and potential donors to evaluate these conflicting obligations and to document the criteria for making such decisions.

It is equally important for an institution to have benchmarks against which to measure performance. Institutions need to understand the expectations of the profession regarding proper procedures and policies.

No single standard will apply to all institutions or in all cases. For nstance, a business or any private organization may be subject to legal or regulatory obligations to maintain certain records for specific periods of time, but private institutions are not legally mandated to create archives or to make records available for researchers outside the organization. They have an obligation to have a records policy in place that is applied on a regular and consistent basis if they destroy records, but these standards meet their legal obligations. A business archives may be available for internal use only. It is possible that some documents may be designated as permanently confidential or may only be made accessible to designated individuals. This is neither improper nor unethical. Manuscripts and personal papers in archival repositories occupy a middle ground between public and private records. They are subject to the requirements of copyright, intellectual property, and privacy law, but other restrictions on access are discretionary and set by the institution. However, government archives or institutions collecting records of publicly funded entities, whose legal mandate and mission are to preserve public records and provide access to them, are under an obligation to limit restrictions on access to as short a period as is legal and reasonable and to provide equal access to the information in a timely and efficient manner.

In addition to these traditionally understood obligations, the profession needs to consider whether there are other areas of institutional administration where good practice requirements are needed to raise the level of professionalism. Some institutional practices that have ethical implications, but are not typically considered in that context, include

1. The availability of staff and resources necessary to process acquisitions in a timely manner;

2. The availability of proper physical facilities for the storage of holdings both on-site and off-site; and

3. The ability to provide appropriate access to the materials collected.

As the commentary to the 1980 SAA ethical code stated, "Excessive delay in processing materials and making them available for use would cast doubt on the wisdom of the decision of a certain institution to acquire materials, though it sometimes happens that materials are acquired with the expectation that there soon will be resources to process those materials or store them properly. In such cases, archivists must exercise their judgment as to the best use of scarce resources, while seeking changes in acquisition policies or increases in support that will enable them to perform their professional duties according to accepted standards."

It is important for the profession to take a realistic look at the ability of institutions to provide quality facilities and services. Although the facts may, at times, be painful for an institution to face, administrators and archivists should know whether they have the appropriate space, personnel, and other physical and financial resources necessary to properly process, protect, and provide access to collections that they accept or solicit. If current operating resources do not permit an institution to professionally administer the materials in its custody, it should utilize this information to do strategic planning for the future and to explore possibilities for procuring the resources necessary to manage its collections. Once again, the ability to benchmark against other similar institutions would provide archivists with an important and concrete tool to take to their administration and to those who allocate the financial resources.

Carolyn Wallace articulated the issue succinctly in her final comments to the 1980 code. She said, "We have tried to write a code broad enough to apply to all. Some areas have caused great problems. For example, the acquisition of private papers involves matters of great ethical concern to manuscript curators but not at all applicable to government or corporate archivists. In the same way, at the request of business archivists, we omitted the emphasis on serving research needs that many of us stress for our own institutions. We tried to keep in mind the wide variety of repositories that archivists serve, and we hope that members of the Society will do the same as they read and criticize the code."

It seems obvious that the Society of American Archivists, and the profession at large, did take Carolyn Wallace's last comment to heart. There has been no criticism of this homogenizing approach to the determination of ethical principles and their application in practices and procedures. Perhaps the profession needs to revisit this issue. Is there another way of dealing with the effect of institutional diversity in evaluating best professional practices other than choosing to abjure the controversial problems that it presents?

One approach would be to have each of the institutional affiliation sections of SAA create best practice standards to serve the specific needs, functions, and responsibilities of the particular type of institution it represents. The sections would review the primary functions performed by the type of institution and create guidelines for best practices within those functions. That would provide institutions with a set of guides that could be used to evaluate their practices and procedures against accepted professional norms in similar repositories. Those standards probably would need to have the final approval of the Standards Board to become formally adopted.

It is interesting to note that the American Association of Museums handles this problem by requiring each of its institutional members to write and adopt their own codes of ethics. This process increases the involvement of the administration and staff in establishing policies and procedures and embeds them in the museum's daily practice. The institutional awareness of strengths and weaknesses derived from this self-evaluative process is important because it forces the museum to review priorities and to commit to a level of performance that reflects the ideals and standards of the profession.

Chapter Three

LAW VERSUS ETHICS

L aw and ethics are not synonymous, nor do they always complement one another. It is possible for an action to be legal, but clearly unethical. For example, what if a senator accepts a large campaign contribution from an organization that has important regulatory legislation pending before a congressional committee that the senator chairs, with the implicit understanding that he is sympathetic to the organization's interests and that the organization's lobbyists will have easy access to the aides of the other committee members to make their case? No laws have been broken, but there is, at least, the appearance of a conflict of interest that could be interpreted as influence peddling.

It also is possible for an action to be ethical, but illegal. For example, a doctor might disclose information about a birth mother to an adoptee in a state where all adoption records are permanently sealed by law. The adoptee is pregnant and needs to know her family's medical history because her fetus shows indications of a hereditary problem for which there is no definitive testing, and family medical history can help her physician to save the baby. It is not legal for the doctor to give her any information, but if he believes the life and health of the fetus are in jeopardy, he is making an ethical choice to disclose information that may help to save the baby's life.

Legal and ethical courses of action do sometimes conflict, forcing individuals to make a choice. In doing so, however, it is a matter of personal conscience, and the individual must be prepared to face the consequences of his or her action. Archivists, like all professionals, are expected to know and obey all relevant laws. The major areas of law pertinent to the archival profession include copyright and intellectual property, freedom of information, privacy and confidentiality, and replevin.

Privacy and confidentiality are the areas of law that most affect archival decision making. Though they are matters of law, privacy and confidentiality also are treated as ethical concerns. Point VII of the "Code of Ethics" says that "Archivists respect the privacy of individuals who created, or are the subjects of, documentary materials of long-term value, especially those who had no voice in the disposition of the materials." The commentary goes on to say, "Subject to applicable laws and regulations, they weigh the need for openness and the need to restrict privacy rights to determine whether release of records or information from records would constitute an invasion of privacy."

United States citizens believe that they have a greater right to privacy than is actually enacted in law. As Gary and Trudy Peterson point out in the SAA publication *Archives and Manuscripts: Law*, "Exactly what privacy means is a little hard to define. . . . The Constitution does not explicitly state that there is a constitutionally protected right to privacy, but many of the provisions of the Bill of Rights do safeguard privacy." The Petersons explain that, "Privacy in its simplest terms, is the right of an individual to be let alone, to live a life free from unwarranted publicity. The violation or invasion of privacy is legally a tort, or civil wrong." [9]

The standard legal textbook on torts—The Law of Torts by William Prosser—lists four basic forms of invasion of privacy recognized in law: (1) intrusion upon the individual's seclusion or solitude, or into his or her private affairs; (2) public disclosure of embarrassing private facts about the individual; (3) publicity that places the individual in a false light in the public eye; and (4) appropriation, for another person's advantage, of the individual's name or likeness. The courts have held that the right to privacy ends with the individual's death. However, as the Petersons' point out, it is possible that disclosure of information about a dead person could violate the privacy rights of survivors or heirs if it directly related to intrusive or embarrassing facts about them. Confidentiality in law relates to the protection of information disclosed in specific professional relationships between doctor and patient, priest and penitent, and attorney and client; and, in most instances, journalist and his or her source of information. In addition to the legal remedies that exist for violations of confidentiality in these relationships, punishment may come from professional licensing boards.

Under law, businesses have no right of privacy. Privacy is accorded to individuals only. Confidential business information is treated as a property right. Businesses have the right under law to protect trade secrets, proprietary information, trademarks, and patents.

The law offers no protection for information that either is a matter of public record or which the victim voluntarily discloses in a public place.

Traditional archival records present fewer discretionary challenges in dealing with privacy and confidentiality than do manuscripts and personal papers. When dealing with these materials, the archivist may have to advise donors who are unconcerned by, or unaware of, sensitive materials in the papers they are offering that may present problems. In such cases, it is the archivist's responsibility to review the papers with an eye to protection of the privacy of people who have not participated in the donation and may not know that embarrassing or defamatory information about them is contained in the collection.

---

[9] See Gary M. Peterson and Trudy Huskamp Peterson, *Archives and Manuscripts: Law* (Chicago: Society of American Archivists, 1985), 39–40.

On the other hand, an archivist may face a potential donor who is reluctant to make papers available for research because he or she is overzealous about what might be considered sensitive information. A donor may wish to keep papers closed for a longer period than is reasonable without justification beyond a gut feeling that he or she doesn't want the information known and available for research. It is the archivist's responsibility in such cases to attempt to persuade the donor to be more accommodating. Archivists need to reassure donors that they are familiar with the law and will protect privacy rights, but at the same time they must make clear the burden that long-term access restrictions place on an institution. Closing collections forces an archives to sustain the cost of maintaining the papers in appropriate environmental conditions without the benefit of allowing their legitimate use for research that is the institution's mission. It requires additional vigilance and special training of staff to differentiate between open and closed material in collections.

There is no universal blueprint for archivists to follow in making their judgment calls regarding privacy and confidentiality. In the digital age, privacy law may undergo some significant changes to extend certain kinds of privacy protections, especially for financial and medical information that is easily accessible via the Internet. Archivists need to keep up-to-date with changes in legal requirements. When it comes to the issue of restricting information and closing collections, each archivist will have to rely upon his or her own ethical judgment. No single right answer covers all situations. Archivists must weigh the extent to which information compromises the privacy of individuals, the policies of their institution, and potential researchers' rights of access to information. The reasons for an institution to make a legal, but ethically questionable decision to buy, to accept, or to close a particular collection can range from the prestige value in owning that collection to a sense that rejection of the collection, even with unreasonable or unnecessary access restrictions, may jeopardize its preservation. This is a fact of professional life. Questionable practices are not an exception in everyday commerce in our society. Therefore, it is important for archivists to openly discuss these issues. The profession needs to try to define the boundaries beyond which decisions cannot be condoned. It is unpleasant, and even painful, to question whether you or your colleagues knowingly or unwittingly engage in practices that are unprofessional or unethical. However, only through frank analysis of action and motive can one determine if he or she is acting in a manner consistent with the highest ethical standards for the profession. It is ultimately a highly subjective judgment and universal agreement may not be reached.

The other area of law that poses major ethical concerns is recovery of personal property. The Petersons' offer a clear explanation of the law:

A number of actions developed in the common law to recover possession of or obtain damages for the loss of personal property. All property is either real property (real estate) or personal property (personalty). Those actions relating to the recovery of personal property were known as replevin, detinue, and trover. Replevin is an action to recover personal property taken, while detinue is an action to recover personal property detained. An archives would have an action in replevin if a document was taken from the archives and the archives had to sue for its return. An archives would have an action in detinue if the archives loaned a document and the individual or institution to whom it was loaned refused to return it, so the archives had to sue for its return. In either case, the archives would also have the right to recover for any damages incurred by the temporary loss of possession. An action in trover, on the other hand, is for damages for the wrongful taking of personal property; in other words, the archives wants money and not the return of the property.

All states have some legal method for the recovery of personal property. Most states (and the United States) have replaced these common law remedies with some form of statutory ones. All of these remedies, whether common law or statutory, whether replevin, detinue, or trover, have come to be called replevin by archivists. For the purposes of this discussion, we will refer to replevin, even though the term is not technically correct.

To recover in a replevin action, the plaintiff must prove title in itself; the institution must recover on the strength of its title and right to possession of the document rather than on the weakness of its opponent's title and right to possession. In other words, just because the possessor of a document does not have good title to it does not mean that the archives can recover the item; the archives will have to show a right to title and possession. There have been very few reported cases involving replevin of documents; however, the few that there are fall into two categories: replevin of public documents and replevin of private documents.[10]

The Petersons explain that in the case of public documents, replevin will depend upon whether or not the document is a public document and appears to be so on its face. This is important because of the "bona fide purchaser" or "innocent purchaser for value" rule which holds that a purchaser of personal property need not return it if he or she paid a fair price for the item and had a reasonable belief that the seller had a right to sell it, and also that nothing indicated that the purchaser had any reason to question the title to the item.

Private documents present another set of problems for the archives. If they have no notice on their face of ownership, as is the case with most personal papers, title has to be proven by other means. If the purchaser is "bona fide,"

---

[10] Ibid., 91.

recovery may be impossible. Replevin for private documents will revolve around questions of superior title and innocence of the purchaser.

Public acknowledgement of the theft or straying of documents may be embarrassing to institutions because it reveals security weaknesses or lack of proper control over holdings, and because it involves the expense of a legal proceeding. Nonetheless, institutions have a moral obligation to seek replevin. Ethically they are obligated to protect and preserve their holdings and ensure their integrity.

The Petersons set the following criteria for public institutions to seek replevin:

1. Every effort should be made to recover documents, regardless of value or significance, if the items clearly were removed illegally.

2. Significant documents that should be in public custody always should be sought.

3. When the missing document is available to the public in a research facility, the government should insure that it will be so in perpetuity and may decide to seek a copy of it instead of the original.

4. Privately held documents not available for public use should be made available for research. If this is not possible, either a copy or the original should be sought to ensure public access. [11]

In the case of private documents, the appropriate ethical response is for the parties involved to negotiate a settlement. Litigation and replevin should be viewed as a last resort. The Petersons' wisely suggest that a copy of a document can serve as well as an original for research and legal purposes. If the innocent purchaser is another archival repository, the purchaser has an ethical obligation to accommodate the original institution. Though legally such a purchaser is not obliged to return the original document, ethically it should do so and try to negotiate the right to keep a copy.

---

[11] Ibid., 92–93.

Chapter Four

CASE STUDIES OF ETHICAL PROBLEMS

The following case studies are intended to promote discussion in classrooms and in workshops about the profession's ethical principles, rules of professional conduct, and suggested institutional best practices.

The arrangement is topical by the major issue addressed in each case. The case study resolutions examine the facts and relate the problem to the pertinent section(s) of the Society of American Archivists' "Code of Ethics." The solutions look at the motive or intent of the parties involved and attempt to reconcile conflicts between ethics and personal morality. The solutions provided for the problems are intended to be reasonable and equitable. However, they may not be the only acceptable resolutions to the conflicts.

As in real life, the case studies do not have single, simple answers that can be applied to all situations. Readers should remember that every problem encountered in their professional life has its own set of facts and characters reacting to the unique circumstances that have led to the problem.

The writing of the case studies was a collaborative effort. I thank each of the contributors, Timothy Ericson, Mark Greene, Leon Miller, Mark Shelstad, Robert Sink, and Robert Spindler, for their assistance.

The reader may wonder why all the case studies are set in the fictitious Sagamore County. It is intended to emphasize that although based on experience, the case studies do not refer to real persons or institutions. Sagamore County was a creation of Timothy Ericson for discussions of ethics with his classes at the University of Wisconsin-Milwaukee. Sagamore County has now taken on a life of its own. I placed all of the case studies somewhere in this mythical locale that is filled with archives and archivists, all facing daunting challenges to their personal and professional integrity.

Users of the case studies are encouraged to frankly discuss the cases and their suggested resolutions. They should bring to bear their own personal experiences and personal ethical principles, along with knowledge of the principles espoused in the SAA "Code of Ethics."

Case Studies

APPRAISAL OF COLLECTIONS
AND COLLECTION POLICIES

Case One
Timothy Ericson, Contributor

You have been working for almost a year as an employee of the Sagamore Regional Archives Center (SRAC). You have a cooperative agreement with the Sagamore County Historical Society (SCHS) whereby its manuscripts are administered by SRAC although SCHS retains title.

During the past year you became acquainted with Harris Miller, a SCHS member, who regularly brings in historical materials ranging from postcards and historical photographs to books on local history and small manuscript collections that relate to the history of the community. The materials he donates are added to the SCHS collection. His only request is that you must keep an accurate record of all of his donations.

Just before Christmas, Miller comes in with another box of materials. He announces that this is the last donation for this year. He tells you that your predecessor customarily extended to him the courtesy of making an "informal" estimate of the value of his donations in case the IRS questioned him about his deduction for "charitable contributions" to SCHS. He wonders whether you might do him the same favor. It would mean a lot to him—he isn't terribly worried about being able to deduct the full value of his donation, so he doesn't mind if you are very conservative in your estimate. All he wants is a short letter signed by you that he can present if he is audited.

What legal and/or ethical issues are at stake here?

How will you handle this request?

The commentary to Section IV of the "Code of Ethics" says, "In accordance with regulations of the Internal Revenue Service and the guidelines accepted by the Association of College and Research Libraries, archivists should not appraise, for tax purposes, donations to their own institutions. Some archivists are qualified appraisers and may appraise records given to other institutions."

The materials in question are not the property of your institution. They belong to the Sagamore County Historical Society. Therefore, it was not improper for your predecessor to give an informal estimate to Mr. Miller. However, the question is whether you are qualified to do so. If not, you should suggest to Mr. Miller that you will give him a letter that indicates the volume and type of material that he donated during the year, and he can get an appraisal of worth from a qualified appraiser or he can give the material his own informal estimate of worth that is in line with previous estimates. If the IRS questioned him on this estimate, he would then need to back it up with an appraisal from a qualified appraiser.

Case Two
Timothy Ericson, Contributor

An alumnus, and big donor to the college where you work, has offered to donate his papers to your archives. He is an amateur historian, and over the years he has spent a lot of research time in your archives. You have become good friends, but you have observed that the gentleman has some eccentric qualities.

The collection is approximately ten cubic feet of correspondence, some of his research files, records relating to his college years, and a voluminous amount of material relating to a personal lawsuit he was engaged in several years ago.

The chair of the history department accepted this donation on your behalf—in part to stop the alumnus, his former student, from pestering him about the donation. He did this with the knowledge and acquiescence of the director of the library, your boss.

You receive the deed of gift for the donation that was negotiated by the library director. It specifies, among other stipulations, that the papers are restricted for a hundred years from the date of acquisition and that only you are permitted to do the processing or have access to the material.

What do you do about this donation?

Section IV of the "Code of Ethics" says, "Archivists discourage unreasonable restrictions on access or use, but may accept as a condition of acquisition clearly stated restrictions of limited duration and may occasionally suggest such restrictions to protect privacy. Archivists faithfully observe all agreements made at the time of transfer."

You are stuck with the material because the director of the library agreed to accept the collection and its stipulated restrictions. Since the library director may be unfamiliar with the "SAA Code of Ethics for Archivists," you should discuss your reservations about the restriction on this collection with the director.

You can point out that a hundred-year restriction on access is, in your opinion, excessive for this material. You should indicate that such a restriction appears to violate the code of professional ethics and is questionable from an administrative point of view because storage space in the archives is limited: these ten cubic feet of papers will just gather dust for a hundred years. The stipulation that you are the only person who may process and have access to the collection presents other problems. If you become ill, incapacitated, or if you take another job, this clause in the agreement would require modification.

More importantly, you should ask that, in the future, the archivist must be included in all negotiations with donors for collections. It is important that signed donor agreements are reasonable and enforceable, or they may cause problems for the institution in the future.

Because you and the donor have a good relationship that has been built up over time, you can ask your director for permission to discuss modification of the agreement with the donor. The papers regarding the lawsuit probably should have access restrictions, depending on the nature of the suit and the sensitivity of the information disclosed. Again, depending on the nature of these records, you may want to suggest that the donor reconsider donation of the material relating to the lawsuit if it was purely a personal suit and the materials have no long-term research value. Your suggestion to him can be based on sensitivity about disclosure of the facts in the case. The other papers, including research material and records relating to his college career, probably do not warrant being restricted for a hundred years, and since he spends time in the archives, he may understand why this information ought to be available for use if it does not present other sensitivity problems. As for the correspondence, it needs to be looked at to determine its exact nature. Are these copies of letters that Miller sent or letters he received? Are they love letters, business letters, or a mix of personal and professional correspondence? Is there anything of a sensitive or confidential nature in the letters? Nothing can be determined about the correspondence until the archivist has appraised the material.

Case Three
Timothy Ericson, Contributor

You are the archivist at Sagamore State University. A faculty member suggests that you solicit the papers of Winthrop D. Irving, a recently deceased writer of mysteries who received his undergraduate degree at your university in 1938. His daughter is now a faculty member in the chemistry department, which is another factor in the placement of his papers at your university. Your collecting policy permits collecting the papers of alumni. The elder Irving taught for more than thirty years (1950–1980) at Union College in Massachusetts. The papers have some information about Irving's student years, but deal primarily with his teaching and writing career from 1953 to 1983. You know that his work is well regarded because his daughter showed you a recent letter of solicitation from Union College describing its own collection of departmental records and unpublished manuscripts documenting aspects of his years there. In addition, you know that the Archives of Modern Mystery Writers recently has become interested in acquiring Irving's papers. Unfortunately, the collection is huge—eight hundred cubic feet (Irving saved everything!) and his daughter wants it moved soon because she has sold the house where it is stored. You are a one-person shop and you have no idea when, if ever, you will be able to process the collection. The daughter wants to retain literary rights for the manuscripts she holds.

What should you do and why?

Section III of the "Code of Ethics" says, ". . . [Archivists] do not compete for acquisitions when competition would endanger the integrity or safety of documentary materials of long-term value, or solicit the records of an institution that has established an archives. They cooperate to ensure the preservation of materials in repositories where they will be adequately processed and effectively utilized." The commentary to this section of the code goes on to say, "Because personal papers document the whole career of a person, archivists encourage donors to deposit the entire body of materials in a single archival institution."

As a one-person operation you do not have the staff, facilities, or budget to deal with a collection of this size. Moreover, you know that Union College already has some of Irving's papers and has expressed an interest in this material.

You should explain to the daughter your reasons for not wanting to accept this collection unless she could guarantee you the resources to process and house it properly. You should suggest to her that Union College, which already has some of her father's papers, would be a good choice as a repository. She should contact the college immediately and respond to its request for the collection, including mentioning her desire to retain literary property rights. She can stress that she is anxious to donate the collection as soon as possible. To maintain good relations with the daughter, you can suggest that you will help her to box up her father's papers and to send them in an appropriate way to Union College if the archives there is still interested in taking them. If Union College does not want the papers for any reason, then you can suggest that she contact the Archives of Modern Mystery Writers as another suitable repository for this collection.

Case Four
Timothy Ericson, Contributor

You have just acquired the personal papers of the Sagamore Family, once very prominent in the community. No living family members remain in the area. Mr. and Mrs. Sagamore died many years ago. The papers came into your possession via an attorney who was acting on behalf of a small foundation that was established in the family's name. The foundation is in the process of disposing of various personal property and real estate in the area.

All of the details concerning the transfer have not yet been worked out. The only living family member, a cousin, is very old and now lives full time in Florida. She will need to sign the final deed of gift, although the attorney does not anticipate any problems with this transaction. In fact, he anticipates making a grant of $10,000 to your archives to help with the processing of the papers.

The collection contains the usual array of family documents: correspondence, legal papers, and papers relating to the large retail company that the family established and later sold. The generation documented in the papers lived in a world of inherited wealth and a good deal of their time was spent enjoying the fruits of their parents' labors. There are voluminous and detailed scrapbooks from world cruises and an exceptionally large and diverse assortment of photographic records. The family patriarch was an amateur photographer and quite gifted at this work. He set up an extensive photo lab in his home and purchased a wide array of photographic equipment. He did much of his own developing and printing. He took movies of their trips and did some nature photography. He also did some "art" photography for which he hired ostensibly "professional" nude models to pose for him. The collection includes some excellent business-related records.

You did not have time to survey the collection extensively before taking delivery, but now you are concerned. In going through the correspondence, you have discovered several letters that appear to be blackmailing the patriarch because of the content of some of his art photographs. The letters are unsigned, but there are ample clues to the identity of the blackmailer. He is another well-known resident of the community who is still alive. He has a reputation as a ne'er-do-well who suddenly came into unexplained wealth. Neither the one surviving cousin nor the attorneys for the foundation know about the photographs and the letters.

What are your legal and ethical obligations regarding these materials?

How will you handle the situation?

The commentary to Section IV of the code says, "Many potential donors are not familiar with archival practices and do not have even a general knowledge of copyright, provision of access, tax laws, and other factors that affect the donation and use of archival materials. Archivists have the responsibility for being informed on these matters and passing all pertinent and helpful information to potential donors. Archivists usually discourage donors from imposing conditions on gifts or restricting access to collections, but they are aware of sensitive materials and do, when necessary, recommend that donors make provision for protecting the privacy and other rights of the donors themselves, their families, their correspondents, and associates."

In this case, the archivist should contact the attorney for the foundation that is handling the transfer of this collection and tell him that neither he nor the family cousin appears to be aware of the sensitive and incriminatory materials in the collection. You can suggest that as the legal representative for the family, he should come and review these materials on the cousin's behalf.

Although it is not the archivist's job to summarily remove material from a collection, and it would be possible for the archivist to restrict access to portions of the collection because of their sensitive nature, in this case it is prudent to allow the lawyer to make a determination of the best way to handle these items. The nude photographs might be shocking to some people, but more importantly, you do not know what agreement Mr. Sagamore made with his models as to the use of their images. If they did not give permission for their photographs to be shown publicly, then it would be a violation of their rights to give the public access to them.

The signed letters that you interpret as possibly blackmailing Mr. Sagamore present another problem. The author of the letters owns the rights to them. His permission would be needed to authorize you to make them available to users while he is still alive. He could sue you. If he were dead, his descendents probably would have objections to the disclosure of the alleged blackmail letters.

It will be up to the attorney, the foundation, and the cousin to decide if this material should be removed from the donation or if it should remain with restrictions on access.

Case Five
Mark Greene, Contributor

You are the curator of manuscripts for a midwestern state historical society. By state statute, the contents of bank safety deposit boxes are forfeited to the state commerce department as abandoned property if the owners fail to pay rent and cannot be located by the bank using certain prescribed methods. The same statutes give the historical society a right to acquire for its collections the contents of any of these boxes deemed to have historical value. So, every ten years or so, the department of commerce invites historical society curators to look through the contents of several hundred safety deposit boxes from all over the state.

This year, amid much realia of concern only to the museum curators, you discover the following three items. The first is a batch of letters received by a student at one of the state's private colleges in the 1970s from several of his high school classmates in an adjoining state. These letters contain extensive references to illegal activities the students carried out, from petty larceny to buying and selling drugs. From the letters it appears that the recipient himself was under investigation for sending marijuana through the U.S. mail. The recipient of these letters is clearly identifiable (though discarding the envelopes would leave only his first name and the college he attended as clues to his identity), as are some of the writers (those who signed their full names). All these individuals would be in their forties now (if still living). The letters provide what is, to your knowledge, the only documentation (outside court records and newspaper reports) of the teenage drug culture in the Midwest. You know researchers would use the collection.

Do you take the collection?

Section VII of the "Code of Ethics" says, "Archivists respect the privacy of individuals who created, or are the subjects of, documentary materials of long-term value, especially those who had no voice in the disposition of the materials." The commentary for this section goes on to say, "Subject to applicable laws and regulations, they [archivists] weigh the need for openness and the need to restrict privacy rights to determine whether release of records or information from records would constitute an invasion of privacy."

The individuals who received and wrote these letters are entitled to their privacy, so it is preferable not to take this collection. However, if there is reasonable justification to save this collection because of its research value, it only could be done if, before allowing access, you removed all individual identifiers by blacking out their names, the name of their school, and any other information that would lead to their identification.

The second item you discover is the early 1980s diary of a professor at a different state college. The diary was written in the form of letters to the married woman he was having an affair with (a staff member at the college). The diary contains extensive information about the course of the affair, the machinations they went through to keep it a secret, and finally the results of having been discovered. The diary writer is identifiable (a quick check of routine sources reveals that he is still employed at the college). The identity of the woman is less readily identifiable. As with the first collection, this diary represents documentation that you are certain will never be available to your repository again—a primary source account of an extramarital affair. Social historians could make excellent use of it.

Do you take the diary?

What are the ethical and legal issues involved?

The same principles apply as in the previous case. These individuals are entitled to their privacy. There was no intent to make the contents of this diary public knowledge. There is no legitimate scholarly purpose in revealing the details of an extramarital affair. You should not take the diary.

The third interesting collection in the safety deposit boxes is the papers of a young soldier from your state who died in Vietnam of heat stroke. The collection is primarily correspondence to and from the soldier while he was at Marine boot camp. The letters are from his girlfriend in your state, his estranged mother in another midwestern state, and his father in your state. There are a few letters from the soldier to his father. When the young man died, his incoming letters were presumably sent home to his father with his other effects. The collection also includes the photos the soldier carried with him (wrapped in tinfoil and plastic) and the contents of his wallet. The photos include two semi-nude snapshots of a young woman, presumably the soldier's girlfriend. Neither the photos nor the letter readily identifies the woman beyond her first name and city of residence. The historical society has very few collections of papers of Vietnam War vets, and none with the intimacy of a set of personal effects. Moreover, your museum is planning an exhibit on the war.

Do you take the collection?

The soldier is dead and by law the right to privacy dies with him. The letters do have a legitimate research value. You accept the collection, but must be sensitive to the privacy of the young woman involved as she presumably is still alive. If the letters contain intimate details that would be embarrassing or compromising to any parties referred to in the contents, then those letters should be restricted until the death of the individuals involved. The seminude photographs have no research value and would be an invasion of privacy of the woman in the picture. They should be disposed of because they were and are an extremely intimate matter between the soldier and his girlfriend. They do not need to be viewed by anyone using the collection. You should make note that such photographs existed and have been removed from the collection. Acknowledgement of their existence is sufficient information for users of the collection.

Case Six
Mark Shelstad, Contributor

The Rock River Historical Society (RRHS) has hired you as a new archivist on its staff. RRHS is a small but active institution, which is funded by both the town of Rock River and the Sagamore County government. It now has a staff of twelve full-time employees—evenly split between administration, the museum, and the archives. One archivist is responsible for accessioning and processing all of the collections with the assistance of two volunteers. The second archivist handles all reference and outreach activities. You will focus on acquisitions and donor relations.

Your first week is spent on orientation—looking at the society's policies, procedures, and programs, and familiarizing yourself with the collections.

The RRHS collections have been acquired over a seventy-year period. A review of the history of the collecting policy shows that the society has made informed and educated decisions about its acquisitions. Its collection policy has made wise use of resources and is focused on the early pioneers in the county; agriculture and agribusiness in the community; and other local business-related collections, including the papers of important figures in the county's economic development.

The RRHS traditionally has worked closely with both the State Archives and the local Rock River College archives. It has arranged for local court records and municipal records to be sent to the State Archives and has referred potential donors to the college's archives when the papers dealt with alumni and faculty.

The college's archives has shared an interest in agribusiness records because of its agribusiness curriculum and the fact that many alumni live and work in the area. Recently however, due to budget cuts, the college fired its professional archivist. A volunteer, an alumnus who is a retired librarian, now staffs the college's archives. RRHS and a number of influential alumni protested this move. The college president has agreed to reconsider this decision if money can be raised to support the program.

As a first activity after your orientation week, the director of RRHS wants you to meet with a potential donor, Robert Hoffman. Hoffman is a graduate of Rock River College. He is a former head of the State Office of Agriculture, who now has a major agribusiness-consulting firm. The director would like an appraisal of the Hoffman collection and recommendations about whether RRHS should acquire these papers.

You discover that there are over a hundred cubic feet of materials, including files on nearly every business in the area involved in agriculture. Hoffman's personal papers and business records document the county's rise as a leading agricultural research and development site. Approximately twenty cubic feet of the materials are personal papers relating to Hoffman's career with the Office of Agriculture.

During your meeting, Hoffman reveals that Rock River College and the State Archives are also interested in his papers. The State Archives wants only the papers related to his work with the Office of Agriculture. The president of the college is trying to convince Hoffman to give the college his papers and to endow the archives, which would then be named in his honor. He won't take the papers unless Hoffman is willing to pay, at least, for their processing and storage.

Hoffman asks for your opinion about what he should do. He also asks for a meeting with RRHS's director to discuss his options.

How should you respond to Hoffman?

What are the legal and ethical issues for you and RRHS?

The code's Section III on collecting policies and the accompanying commentary are pertinent to this situation. The code says, "Archivists arrange transfers of records and acquire documentary materials of long-term value in accordance with their institutions' purposes, stated policies, and resources. They do not compete for acquisitions when competition would endanger the integrity or safety of documentary materials of long-term value, or solicit the records of an institution that has established an archives. They cooperate to ensure the preservation of materials in repositories where they will be adequately processed and effectively utilized."

The commentary says, "Among archivists generally there seems to be agreement that one of the most difficult areas is that of policies of collection and the resultant practices. Transfers and acquisitions should be made in accordance with a written policy statement, supported by adequate resources and consistent with the mission of the archives. Because personal papers document the whole career of a person, archivists encourage donors to deposit the entire body of materials in a single archival institution. This section of the code calls for cooperation rather than wasteful competition, as an important element in the solution of this kind of problem.

Institutions are independent and there will always be room for legitimate competition. However, if a donor offers materials that are not within the scope of the collecting policies of an institution, the archivist should tell the donor of a more appropriate institution. When two or more institutions are competing for materials that are appropriate for any one of their collections, the archivist must not unjustly disparage the facilities or intentions of others. As stated later, legitimate complaints about an institution or an archivist may be made through proper channels, but giving false information to potential donors or in any way casting aspersions on other institutions or other archivists is unprofessional conduct.

It is sometimes hard to determine whether competition is wasteful. Because owners are free to offer collections to several institutions, there always will be duplication of effort. This kind of competition is unavoidable. Archivists cannot always avoid the increased labor and expense of such transactions."

In this case, the code is explicit about what you should do in this situation. You need to tell Mr. Hoffman that it is not your place to comment on the other institutions that are interested in his papers. It is up to him to decide where to place them. You should tell him that the Rock River Historical Society is interested in accepting the collection because it fits directly into its collecting interests and complements other holdings. You should mention that generally it is better to keep a collection of personal papers together and not to divide them between institutions on a topical basis. You should suggest that it is a good idea for him to discuss his options with the director of RRHS.

On the matter of whether you should consider the plight of Rock River College and how this deposit could save the archives, it would be considered unprofessional for you to discuss the college's financial difficulties. However, the college has shown that the archives is vulnerable through the firing of the archivist when decisions had to be made about resources. There is no guarantee that Mr. Hoffman's deposit of his papers and his financial support for their processing and storage would restore the position of a professional archivist or be sufficient to maintain operation of the archives. You should discuss this with the director and let him decide if there is an appropriate way to bring these issues to the potential donor's attention.

Case Seven
Mark Shelstad, Contributor

Your first professional position is as archivist for Bosler Community College. Bosler was founded in 1946. It now has two thousand students and a hundred faculty members. The college archives was established in 1965. The former archivist, who set up the archives, has just retired. The archivist reports to the college librarian. The staff consists of a full-time assistant archivist and a part-time work/study student.

Your first days at work reveal that the archives has no collection policy and that there is no central focus to what has been acquired. No systematic effort has been made to acquire the administrative records of the college. The archives has some scattered records from admissions and a few yearbooks, but no other student records. There is a smattering of correspondence of the presidents of the college. The most complete run of records is for the last five years of promotion and tenure for the faculty.

Approximately three hundred feet of manuscript collections appear to be sixty different small collections of various natures, including family papers, manuscripts of a local author, papers of two local ladies clubs, the records of the local daily newspaper that ceased publication in 1970, and a collection of railroad photographs. About 250 feet of this material is unprocessed or poorly processed without completed finding aids. This backlog presents a real challenge to your small staff.

The policy has been to create a box/folder list when materials were acquired. This list was the official receipt to the donor and often was accompanied by a financial appraisal of the value of the donation. The archives would then send printed materials to the library for the stacks or separate out clippings for the library's vertical subject files.

Correspondence with donors reveals that the archives used several different letterheads indicating that about six different "special subject centers" within the archives that maintained curatorial control over the collections. Used to entice donors, the "centers" were not really operational or administrative entities.

You decide to sample the collections and find that many of them have extremely limited research value. Conversations with the staff show that the archives gets little use by the college community or outside researchers.

Access is a concern. There are no traditional archival finding aids. A card catalog in the reading room purports to do item-level subject description, but does not include all of the processed collections.

The librarian has charged you with gaining physical and intellectual control over the all of the collections, improving access and finding aids, creating a collection policy that will encompass all of the current holdings, and setting up schedules for the college records. At the same time, the librarian says there is little or no chance for additional staff. Moreover, you are not to contact any previous donors to request funding help. Meanwhile, two previous donors have contacted you about donating additional materials for a financial valuation.

What is your response to the librarian?

What are your ethical responsibilities to the college?

What are your ethical responsibilities to donors?

Your first job obviously presents enormous challenges to a new archivist. You need to be honest in your discussions with the librarian. You have to tell him that there are no easy, cheap, quick fixes for long-standing problems. You should prepare a strategic plan for the archives for five years. You need to prioritize the work that needs to be tackled to gain intellectual control over the material now housed in the archives and to create proper finding aids to provide access for research and use of these materials.

The first priority is to write a collection policy for the archives that will determine what kinds of documents you will seek and what you will accept in future donations. The next step will be to create records schedules for the college that will establish the archives as the permanent repository for selected records. While you want to dramatically improve the perception of the archives as an important resource for information and set up professionally accepted procedures for its operations, you must be realistic in what you can accomplish within your budget, staff limits, and support. You need a work plan and timeline with goals and objectives that you know that you can meet.

With your strategic plan, work plan, and timeline in hand, you should meet with the librarian and discuss the future of the archives. You can suggest that present holdings need to be re-appraised for their research value. You can use this information to seek outside grant funding for their processing and the creation of finding aids for these collections. It will be a step-by-step process to build a sustainable program that meets the needs of the college and potential researchers.

Your ethical responsibility to the college is, as the "Code of Ethics" states in its conclusion, Section XIII, "...[to] work for the best interests of [your] institution and...profession and endeavor to reconcile any conflicts by encouraging adherence to archival standards and ethics."

As for the two donors indicating they will donate more materials in exchange for a monetary evaluation of the items, you need to tell them that the "SAA Code of Ethics" says that it is unethical for an archivist to give monetary appraisal of materials headed for his or her own collection. You can provide the donors with a signed statement of the items that have been donated, and they can make their own approximate valuation of worth or can get an outside evaluation from another archivist qualified to appraise the collections.

Case Eight
Mark Shelstad, Contributor

The Sagamore State University Archives and Special Collections Department has a long tradition of acquiring manuscript collections. The tradition stems from its former director, who firmly believed in collecting the materials first before concerning himself with the appraisal, processing, and access. Following the director's retirement, the university librarian seeks an outside professional opinion about the archives program and the value of the collections. She hires a consultant to provide an evaluation and recommendations. The consultant is provided with the current collection policy and procedures and the guide to the collections. He also will have the opportunity to talk with the archives' staff.

The consultant finds that the archives needs additional space, that the current collection policy is seldom used, and that about one-third of the collections have little research value or are not appropriate to the institution. However, overall, the collections provide a great resource for the university and its research community.

The consultant learns that the use of a deed of gift form for outside collections was implemented only recently. Many of the donations are well documented, but for some critically important collections, legal ownership cannot be substantiated.

Letters in the donor files are primarily concerned with shipping and packing instructions, updates on the archives' activities, and holiday greetings. The informal letters often contain the phrase that "the archives undoubtedly is willing to keep everything" that the donor sends. Similarly, the donor letters are vague in regard to restrictions on access to collections. The accession records may indicate that a collection is restricted, but there is no correspondence in the donor files that discusses or describes the terms of the access restrictions. In other cases, sensitive or confidential materials are available to researchers without evidence that access was discussed with the donors.

The consultant makes several recommendations to the university to streamline the collecting policy, reappraise some of the collections for possible deaccessioning, and attempt to establish legal ownership for the collections with no documentation.

The consultant advises the university that it should consider the public relations/political consequences of deaccessioning on the university archives' reputation. The report suggests that the university can consider returning material to the donor, transferring it to another suitable repository, selling it through a public auction house, or destroying it. Reappraisal and deaccessioning are crucial because of space considerations, budget, and the need to create a collection policy that better serves the university and the research community.

The consultant's report is well received by the university. The president and the university librarian are particularly intrigued by the option of selling a large collection of motion picture posters. This type of poster recently has escalated in value as a collectible according to a national news program. The proceeds would generate badly needed money for operating funds and salaries.

The collection was acquired from a now-deceased alumnus who operated the local movie theater for four decades. It is unclear from the correspondence if he gave the posters to the university or thought that it was storing them for him under more appropriate conditions than he could provide. Although they were not very valuable at the time they came to the university, the letters from the donor demonstrate that he thinks they would be worth a great deal some day. He has a son living in town who would learn about any sale of the collection.

What are the university's and the archives' responsibility to the donors?

Should they proceed with the deaccessioning and auction of the movie poster collection?

Having signed donor agreements that specify ownership of the collection, all rights in the material and any restrictions on access are legal responsibilities of the archives. Not having such a clear statement of donor intent places the movie poster collection in limbo status. The archives needs to seek legal advice before making any decision about deaccessioning and auctioning off the collection. The ethical thing to do would be to go to the donor's son and explain that the status of his father's donation needs to be clarified. That may or may not be the advice of the attorney representing the university, and the ultimate decision of how to proceed will be made by the university president and the university librarian. You should remind them that the son may be aware of his father's intent and that it needs clarification. If the son believes that the movie posters are his property or expects them to be returned to him if the archives wishes to dispose of them, then the university can expect that he will seek legal advice and may sue the university. The negative publicity, whatever the outcome of the suit, will damage the university and the archives' reputation. It will affect future donations of material. So, the university should make every effort to do the right thing.

Case Nine
Robert Sink, Contributor

The Sagamore County Historical Society (SCHS) has acquired the records of the local American Nazi Party chapter. As assistant archivist, you have arranged for two members of the staff to pack the materials and transport them to the archives.

While loading the cartons, the staff members see some printed material with images that they consider to be extremely offensive. They walk out in protest and complain to the archivist about the repository acquiring such material. The archivist explains to them that SCHS has made the decision to acquire these materials based on their historical research value and that staff members should return and do their job.

They are so upset at the offensive nature of this material that they give an interview to the local newspaper. The publicity leads to the donor threatening to withdraw from the gift agreement. Your supervisor explains to the press the reasons for preserving this type of material for future research and reprimands the staff members for violating the institution's confidentiality agreement.

Eventually the situation disappears from the news. The donor is mollified and the material is transferred to the archives. The collection is accessioned and prepared for processing.

What sort of policies should the archives adopt to cover this type of situation in the future?

The personal morality of the two staff members sent to pack up the Nazi material was deeply offended, and they were correct in expressing their concerns to their supervisor, the archivist. Rather than ordering them to go back and pack up the materials, the archivist should have explained to them, as he did, the reason why the archives had acquired this collection. Then he should have expressed an understanding of their perspective while emphasizing that this material has significant research value and should not be censored because it is offensive. If the explanation did not satisfy the employees' moral qualms about the records, then the archivist and assistant archivist should have arranged to go back and finish the packing themselves.

The staff members were unprofessional in going to the press without first talking the matter over at greater length with the archivist. If they were still unsatisfied, then they should have taken the matter up with the archivist's supervisor. They could have asked to be relieved of any responsibility for dealing with these materials on the grounds that they offended their moral principles. They have a responsibility to uphold the reputation of the institution; they should not have embarrassed the institution by going to the press and giving the interviews. Moreover, they behaved unethically in violating the confidentiality agreement between the archives and the donor. In the future, the archives should allow staff members to exempt themselves from working with materials that offend their personal ethics because it is impossible for individuals to deal impartially and without bias in such cases. Violating confidentiality agreements and restrictions on access should be grounds for job probation, and a second offense grounds for dismissal.

Case Ten
Robert Sink, Contributor

You are the institutional archivist at a large bank, which operates a hundred branches around the state and is headquartered in Sagamore Falls. As the archivist, it is your responsibility to appraise all of the records of the bank, including architectural records.

Your city has a strong landmark preservation law, which states that once a building is designated as a landmark neither its interior nor exterior can be altered without the approval of a special committee of the city council. Approval for such alterations is very time consuming and costly to obtain and it is not granted often.

The policy adopted by the board of directors of the bank mandates a vigorous opposition to landmark designation for any of its buildings. One local community council, however, has joined together with a group of preservation professors to nominate the bank's earliest branch building for landmark status. This branch represents the finest existing example of commercial architecture by a nationally known architect.

As you survey the bank's records, you find a cache of original architectural drawings, which obviously have continuing administrative and historical value. Among them are the drawings for the branch proposed for landmark status. You know that the existence of the drawings will make it easier for the preservationists to argue in favor of landmark designation.

What is your ethical responsibility?

What appraisal decision do you make?

Section VI of the "Code of Ethics" dealing with appraisal says, "Archivists protect the integrity of documentary materials of long-term value in their custody, guarding them against defacement, alteration, theft, and physical damage, and ensure that their evidentiary value is not impaired in the archival work of arrangement, description, preservation, and use."

You should keep the drawings because they have historical and evidentiary value. They are the work of a famous architect and should not be destroyed. It is your obligation to let your supervisor know of the existence of these drawings. It is not your obligation to inform the preservationists of their existence unless they specifically ask you for that information. As a private institution, the bank's records are its private property. It has no obligation to make them available to anyone outside of the bank's staff unless the bank is involved in a lawsuit. Depending upon the bank's access policy for the archives, you may or may not give the preservationists access to the records. In many corporate archives it is the legal staff, or a committee composed of executives, that evaluates outside requests for information from the archives. It is not necessarily the responsibility of the archivist to provide access to records to individuals outside of the organization without first determining the nature of their research and whether the bank supports it.

On the other hand, if outside researchers are pursuing access to the records through legal intervention, it is your duty to inform the lawyers of the existence of the records during discovery proceedings.

AN ARCHIVIST'S RESPONSIBILITY TO HIS OR HER EMPLOYING INSTITUTION

Case Eleven
Timothy Ericson, Contributor

You recently have been hired as the archivist at the Sagamore County Historical Society (SCHS). The director has brought you a draft of a grant application that is being submitted to support the creation of a regional preservation program at your facility. She wants your recommendations concerning possible revisions to the final text.

You know that one of the crucial criteria the granting agency uses in determining who receives funding is the continuation of the project after the period of the grant has ended. In addressing the question of continuation, the draft says that while it is "impossible to predict with complete accuracy the future," the SCHS "has every reason to believe that the project will be supported on a continuing basis."

In casual conversations around the SCHS you have heard the director and several of the staff members suggest that this is not at all the case—that the society is primarily interested in obtaining some equipment and a temporary staff member who can do some much needed preservation work with your records in advance of the county centennial.

What will you recommend?

What is your ethical responsibility here?

You should read the grant application carefully and suggest any changes that you believe will improve it as you have been asked to do by the director. When you return the proposal to her with your comments, you should ask if you could speak with her about one point not addressed in your written comments. Your professional and ethical responsibility is to raise the issue and discuss it with the director. You can express your concern that a major critical factor in securing funding is the ongoing commitment to the project. You should tell her that you have overheard comments indicating that the historical society does not intend to continue the project when the grant funding has ended. You note that there is not a promise of continuation in the proposal, but you still are concerned on two counts. One, that in evaluating the grant the readers may pick up on the language used and recognize that it expresses a lack of commitment to continuing the project in the post-grant period, thereby lessening the chances for receiving funding. Two, that failure to continue funding the project after the grant is spent could negatively affect the historical society's competitiveness when applying for other future grants.

COMPLAINTS ABOUT OTHER INSTITUTIONS

Case Twelve
Karen Benedict, Contributor

You are the full-time archivist at Sagamore State College, a two-year junior college. You have a B.A. in history and after being hired for the job four years ago, you attended two workshops on archives administration given by the regional archival association. Three volunteers work for you on a part-time basis. All three of them are retired faculty members with lots of knowledge about the college's history. Your program is supported by the college administration, and you are proud of your accomplishments.

Slippery Elm State College, which is twenty-five miles away, is Sagamore State College's rival for students. It has a larger faculty and a larger student body. Slippery Elm decides it needs to create an archives. The Slippery Elm president asks the Sagamore State president if he can send his new archivist to observe operations at the Sagamore State College Archives for a week to learn more about how things are done there. Your president agrees, and the Slippery Elm State College archivist arrives on your campus. She has a master's degree in history and has done graduate course work in archives. It is clear to you after a short time that she feels superior in her qualifications and is not impressed by your archives. The week is tense, and you are relieved when she returns to Slippery Elm.

In the next few weeks you begin to hear rumors that the Slippery Elm State College archivist is saying disparaging things about you, your volunteer staff, and the quality of your archival holdings. This is distressing information, but you do not know what to do. Should you openly confront her, complain to her administration, or take the high road and ignore her comments? Ultimately the rumors filter through to your president. You are called into a meeting with him. There also are two history faculty members present. You are given a list of questions about the quality of your work that the president and the faculty members have put together based on the comments they have gotten from a variety of people who have heard the disparaging remarks.

What do you do?

You ask to have time to review the questions and to get back to the president and faculty members in a week. It is a no-win situation to become defensive or to denigrate the Slippery Elm State College archivist. You need to carefully evaluate the criticisms to see if any are justified and whether the comments contain any constructive suggestions to improve your program.

At the same time, you are sure that the Slippery Elm archivist has behaved badly. You make a call to one of your former workshop instructors. She tells you that the Society of American Archivists has a "Code of Ethics" and that this kind of behavior is unethical. You download a copy of the "Code of Ethics" from the SAA Web site and see for yourself that it says, "...in any way casting aspersions on other institutions or other archivists is unprofessional conduct."

For the upcoming meeting, you prepare a written response to the questions in the form of a work plan for the things that you and your volunteer staff can do to improve the archives' acquisitions, processing, and accessing procedures. You create a wish list of things that you would like to do, but cannot accomplish within the current budget. You also list the things that you have been able to do in the past four years to establish the archives.

At the meeting, you present your response and indicate that you are willing to continue your education through additional workshops and classes. You present copies of the SAA "Code of Ethics for Archivists" and let them read for themselves the sections on collecting policies and complaints about other institutions that pertain to the situation.

At the end of the meeting, the president commends you for your positive attitude and agrees to do all that he can to continue to support the archives.

COMPETITION FOR COLLECTIONS

Case Thirteen
Timothy Ericson, Contributor

You are the archivist for Sagamore Regional Archives (SRA). One day an acquaintance—a long-time friend of the SRA with whom you have worked on several different projects and public programs—stops by your office.

He is an officer in the MacArthur Society, a local organization founded in 1859, whose membership consists of many prominent community residents with Scottish ancestry.

He explains that a number of years ago (he doesn't recall how many, but quite a few), his organization placed its records in the Sagamore County

Historical Society (SCHS). The records have never been processed and there is not even an inventory of the contents of the boxes. He recently stopped by SCHS to see the records and was told that he would have to stop back another day because it would take some time to locate and bring the records to the archives' reading room.

He further explains that he has heard of others who have donated records to the SCHS and have had to pay to make copies to use their own materials. The SCHS cannot presently locate the deed of gift, if one does exist, and no one recalls the terms of the deposit of the collection with SCHS. The donor tells you that he would like to reclaim the records from SCHS and donate them to your archives. He is only stopping by to ask whether you would accept the MacArthur Society collection if he is successful in having it transferred to your institution. However, if it were necessary for him to go to court to retrieve it, he would like you to serve as an expert witness for the MacArthur Society to explain that SCHS has not fulfilled its obligations in a professional manner.

You would love to have the collection. Your regional archival collection contains a number of similar groups of records from community organizations, many of them ethnic in origin. In fact, this is one of the areas emphasized in your collection development policy and mission statement. The MacArthur Society records would be a great addition to your holdings. You have heard a number of complaints about SCHS in the past few years, but you have no firsthand knowledge of their validity.

Is it ever appropriate to criticize the operations of another archival institution?

How do you work with a potential donor who has had a negative experience with another archives?

It would not be appropriate to criticize SCHS. The code is very clear that it is unprofessional to do so. If you are concerned about the SCHS's performance and have questions or criticisms, they should be addressed to SCHS and its staff.

You can tell your friend that your institution would be interested in the MacArthur Society records if he recovers them from SCHS. You should make clear that it appears he has reasons to be dissatisfied with their performance, but that it is an issue that he must resolve between SCHS and the MacArthur Society. Because you have no firsthand knowledge of SCHS's program; because it is a matter of ethics that you should not publicly criticize the institution; and because your impartiality would be comprised were your institution to be the recipient of the records, you cannot appear as an expert witness if the matter ends up in court. You can suggest that he contact the Society of American Archivists and explain his situation. Perhaps they can recommend a way to resolve the conflict or make suggestions for the appropriate way for him to try to resolve his problem with SCHS. Or you can help him find an impartial expert witness if the matter has to go to court.

Case Fourteen
Timothy Ericson, Contributor

A former U.S. senator who was born and raised in your community has offered your archives a small collection of his personal papers.

The materials relate to his boyhood years, through the time when he graduated from high school and took a job selling life and auto insurance. There are also some materials relating to a project to write an autobiography that he started in retirement (it never was finished). It comprises some excellent material, including a number of very good family photographs.

The senator's political career was sufficiently noteworthy that some years ago the state historical society acquired his congressional papers. However, the state historical society does not have any materials about the senator's boyhood years, or anything from the time following his retirement—nor has it made any effort to acquire such materials.

How do you handle the senator's offer? Will you accept the collection?

If yes, why? If no, why not?

You should tell the senator that you are aware that his congressional papers are at the state historical society and that the archival profession believes it is best practice to keep an individual's papers together in a single institution. Therefore, he should first contact the state historical society and see if it is interested in his personal papers. If it is not, or if the senator does not decide to donate them to the state historical society, then you would be pleased to accept the collection.

Case Fifteen
Leon Miller, Contributor

You are the manuscripts archivist of Mt. Nord College, a midsized private college in rural Sagamore County. Your department specializes in preserving the documentary heritage of the surrounding region. Of special importance to your department are papers and records documenting area folklore and folklore studies, the nationally recognized local crafts movement, and records of organizations sponsoring various local folk, music, and crafts festivals. One of your important donors and supporters is local community leader Ellen Flagler. Ellen is a graduate of Mt. Nord. She has served on the town council and the boards of several area festival organizations, and she currently serves as president of the state folklore society. She also has held every office in your friends' group.

Eight years ago, Ellen donated her personal papers to your repository. Since then she has made additional donations of her papers in installments every year or two. Among the documents that she has not yet given are her scrapbooks. These scrapbooks record her political achievements as well as her work with folklore societies. "I'm keeping those until my grandkids are old enough to look at them," she says.

Also on your campus is a separate, independent manuscripts repository. It specializes in women's studies and was created about four years ago. It gives special emphasis to preserving the papers of women graduates of Mt. Nord College.

The head of that repository, Patricia Hampstead, has a personal research interest in women's scrapbooks. She has made collecting them the special focus of the repository. She also keeps informed about local women's collections and has visited your repository several times to review the Flagler papers.

When Ellen delivers her next installment of papers, she mentions that she ran into Hampstead at church last Sunday. "Pat explained to me how her archives specializes in scrapbooks like mine," Ellen reported. "She said that since I'm a Mt. Nord graduate, my scrapbooks really belong in her archives and I should donate them to her." You are taken aback by this revelation.

How do you respond to Ellen Flagler's statement?

What would your approach be to settling this issue with the head of the rival special collections section?

You tell Ellen that she should be flattered that her scrapbooks are of great interest. You go on to say that the archival profession strongly believes that it is best practice for an individual's personal papers to be together in a single repository and not divided between or among institutions. You explain that her scrapbooks are most meaningful in the context of all of her work that is documented in her papers. Anyone interested in her political achievements and her work to preserve the region's folklore would want to look at her entire collection and not the scrapbooks in isolation. You express willingness to make copies of the scrapbooks, if they are in your collection, should Pat Hempstead want to place copies in her special collections facility for comparative purposes with other scrapbooks. The originals, however, should be in the archives with Ellen's other papers. Yours is the repository that folklore researchers are familiar with and use for their projects.

You call Pat Hempstead and arrange to have lunch with her. During the meal you mention that Ellen Flagler has told you of Pat's interest in her scrapbooks. You tell Pat the same things that you have told Ellen. You let her know that you do not consider yourself in competition with her. You want to do what is best for the records. You repeat your offer to provide her with copies of the scrapbooks if she wants to have them.

You hope that the discussion has persuaded Pat to work with you collaboratively. If she continues to pursue the Flagler material, then your next option is to go to the director of the campus library and share your concerns.

Case Sixteen
Leon Miller, Contributor

You are the special collections librarian at Sagamore A&M, a land-grant school. You require signed deeds of gift to accompany new acquisitions. However, previous heads of your department did not follow that policy, and from the 1950s through the 1980s, special collections routinely acquired collections on deposit without proper paperwork regarding the conditions of deposit and access.

Two years ago, a wealthy resident left the bulk of her estate to the Lake Sagamore Historical Society. Overnight, the small, sleepy society became one of the nation's best-funded local historical organizations. Its board of directors built a research facility and hired a staff to run it, charging it with quickly creating an important archival collection.

You served as an advisor to the historical society during this process. Its new staff members often visited your repository for tours, to pick up tips, and to review your procedures. They also poured through your finding aids, most of which contained short-form provenance statements, such as "these papers were deposited by William B. Godshaw in August 1972" or "the Sagamore County Kiwanis Club donated its records to Special Collections in January 1996."

Several months after the historical society's new facility opened, the sons of William B. Godshaw called you to say the family wished to withdraw Godshaw's papers from your department and donate them to the historical society. You tried to talk with them about the significant resources your university had devoted to preserving their father's papers, but to no avail. Soon thereafter, you began receiving more calls in the same vein. It becomes clear to you that the historical society personnel had used your finding aids to discover which of your collections were on deposit, and then they had systematically solicited the owners to donate their collections to the historical society.

What legal and ethical recourse do you have in resolving this situation?

How do you respond to the Godshaw family?

Will you directly confront the historical society, or seek other ways to deal with the problem?

Naturally, you are very disturbed, but without a signed donor agreement or a deed of gift you are on shaky legal ground. If the family is committed to removing the papers from your archives and placing them in the historical society, you potentially will create more negative repercussions by not cooperating with them than by acquiescing with good grace.

You need to sit down with the director of the library and make sure she is fully aware of what is happening and why. Perhaps she will want to make another appeal to the Godshaw family. However, if the Godshaws pursue this action, then you need to cooperate with them.

You can contact the regional and the national professional associations and make them aware of your problem. Perhaps they would be willing to mount a letter-writing campaign to the historical society protesting its actions as unprofessional and unethical.

Since you were an adviser to the historical society in its early stages, you obviously know the director and the staff there. You should arrange to meet with them and express your dismay at the "raiding" of your holdings. You can try to persuade them that such actions will ultimately redound to their discredit. Their actions can affect the future reputation of the historical society and its relations with potential donors because they have behaved unprofessionally and violated the spirit of the "Code of Ethics for Archivists."

COPYRIGHT

Case Seventeen
Mark Greene, Contributor

You are a staff archivist at the Sagamore State Archives assigned to create a compelling on-line and hard copy exhibit documenting the accomplishments of the recently retired U.S. senator, Cyrus B. Worthington. Although the archives has an excellent selection of Worthington publicity and campaign photographs, it does not have a photo relating to the senator's most notable legislative effort, the Rural Electrification Privatization and Decentralization Act of 1995.

In your frantic last-minute efforts to locate images for the exhibit, you visit the senator's Web site and find a wonderful photo of the senator shaking hands with the current governor Naughton B. Shredding at a press conference announcing the passage of the electrification legislation. The photo is mounted on the Web in high resolution, so it could be downloaded and used to produce a publication-quality photograph that is perfect for your exhibit. The photographer and the source of the photo are not cited for copyright permission or attribution. As you begin to download the image you notice that one of Governor Shredding's staff members is visible, her nametag is legible, and she has her hand on the governor's shoulder as he is shaking hands with the senator.

Should you use the image?

What legal and ethical issues are involved?

If you do decide to use the image, whom must you ask for copyright permission?

Should you retouch the photograph to hide the aide's name or image?

How would you cite the photograph?

If retouched, should it be identified as a photo illustration?

What right of privacy do the people in the photograph have in this case?

If it is the best image for your purposes, then you will want to pursue the possibility of using it. It would be illegal, and therefore unethical as well, to use the image without copyright permission. The copyright rests with the photographer unless this was a work-for-hire job where the photographer was paid and relinquished rights to the work, or if it was the work of a staff photographer in the governor's office. It also may be the work of a press photographer attending the press conference, making the image the property of the newspaper or news service employing him.

You need to contact the senator's Web site manager and find out the identity of the photographer and for whom he or she worked. Then you will need to contact the owner of the copyright for permission to reproduce the image. The photograph should be cited to its original source—the photographer, governor's office, or news media.

As it was taken at a news conference, you do not need to seek the permission of the people in the photograph because it was a public occasion, the image has been published, and you have obtained copyright permission to reproduce it. However, if you want to retouch the photo to eliminate the aide, then you need to ask permission of the copyright holder to alter the image. It should be cited as a photo illustration if the original image is altered.

DEED OF GIFT

Case Eighteen
Timothy Ericson, Contributor

Y ou are the archivist at Sagamore State College. Years ago your archives was given a collection of personal letters of a former college president who served the school during the 1920s until his death in 1929. The letters, love letters between the president and his wife prior to their marriage in 1903, were found in a desk that was taken out of storage in the late 1960s.

The late president's granddaughter, now in her fifties, comes to the archives and announces that she and other family members would like the letters to be returned to her. She states that the family feels that they should have been given the letters when they were first discovered.

The content of the letters is tame with no embarrassing revelations, and indeed they are well written and poetical. Scholars of American culture and literature have said that they provide a fine example of late-nineteenth-and early-twentieth-century courtship and social mores. Still, the granddaughter maintains, it is an embarrassment to the family to make them publicly available.

The letters were deposited in the college's archives years ago before there was much concern with official deeds of gift. A staff member who was there at the time recalls that the letters were offered to the president's daughter, now deceased, who declined them and told the archivist that the archives should keep them. This was, however, an oral agreement. The collection has been processed and is well cared for in acid-free boxes and folders. A member of the faculty published a book on American culture eight years ago that quoted ten of the letters. There also has been more recent use of the materials. A faculty member is using the love letters as the basis for a current campus theater production on the college's history. A graduate student is quoting portions of the letters in her doctoral thesis on courtship traditions for women's studies.

The library director wants your opinion on retaining the letters in the archives.

What is the college's legal position?

Since some letters are already published and therefore available to researchers, does that affect the situation?

Does the granddaughter have legitimate privacy concerns?

The college is on shaky legal ground. The letters were found, not donated by the writer(s). There is no written proof that the president's daughter said that the archives should keep them, and there is no deed of gift or other legal instrument from her making them the property of the college archives.

While some of the letters have been published, and I presume that permission was sought from the archives, it is a problem because the rights do not rest with the college as owner of copyright and literary rights.

Privacy dies with the individual under law. Therefore, the granddaughter does not have a legal privacy right. However, archives and the courts have been sensitive to the privacy of individuals affected by these kinds of disclosures. The description of the case indicates that there are no embarrassing details in the letters, but that they are of literary merit. So, the privacy argument is weak. Nonetheless, without legal custody of the letters, the college has to return them to the granddaughter or persuade her to make a donation of them to the archives.

Case Nineteen
Timothy Ericson, Contributor

You are at a donor's home to complete the acquisition of a large collection of business and family papers. The donor is anxious to complete the transaction because the house has been sold and the closing will take place in a few days. As you are loading the material into your van you are spot checking the boxes, which were packed by movers, to create a rudimentary inventory of the materials. As you do so, you notice several items that are probably quite valuable. Included are several sheets of uncut "wildcat currency" dating from the 1850s, some campaign ribbons from the 1860 election, and a small stamp collection that apparently was started by one of the donor's ancestors. None of the materials are integral to the manuscript materials.

The donor already has signed a deed of gift, which gives you the right to dispose of any unwanted items in whatever way you think best.

Do you bring the valuable items to the attention of the donor?

Why or why not?

Yes, you tell the donor that you notice several valuable items are included with the manuscript materials. You have a moral obligation to be sure that he is aware of all of the items that he is donating.

Although the "Code of Ethics" contains no specific provision to deal with this situation, you always need to be fair and honest in your relations with donors. It may be that the donor does intend for the archives to benefit from any materials that are valuable and can be sold. Your personal integrity and code of moral behavior should lead you to be forthcoming in this situation. Perhaps the archives will benefit from your honesty.

Case Twenty
Mark Greene, Contributor

You have just been appointed as archives director of the Sagamore Falls Historical Society. You are the first archivist ever to be hired and the place is a mess! You see that it will be quite a challenge with the meager budget you have been given.

Along with the archival collections is a large accumulation of artifacts consisting mainly of small items, such as political buttons, medals, souvenirs of various shapes and sizes, postcards, autographed photos of sports celebrities, stamp and coin collections, and the like. What paperwork exists indicates that the material came in with donations of manuscript collections and was separated during processing.

The material is of no use to your archives or to the SFHS; however, some of it is quite valuable. If it was sold, you might be able to purchase some badly needed supplies and equipment, such as a computer and software.

Several deeds of gift relate to the manuscript donations with which the artifacts were included. Unfortunately, the form the SFHS used in the past simply specified that you will "preserve" the material. No mention is made of making further disposition—let alone selling off any part of the donation.

What are the ethical and legal issues that should govern your decision making?

What changes will you make in the policies of your institution in light of this experience?

Poor procedures for acquisition of collections, especially the lack of signed legal instruments for the donation or deposit of holdings, are a major bane of archives and archivists. It is unclear whether or not the documentation that exists specifies which artifacts belong with which collection. If you can make the connection, you should update the paperwork to clearly indicate which artifacts are a part of which donations.

If the facts can be established, then you can go back to the donors and explain the situation. If you are going to dispose of the artifacts and the family wants them back, you should return them. If family members are willing to allow the archives to sell the items and keep the profits, then you should get a signed document that gives the archives permission to make the sale.

If the items are not identifiable as to donor, then you need to consult with your supervisor or the board of directors, and perhaps legal counsel, to make a decision about the best way to handle these items. You can sell them or donate them to another repository that collects these items.

As for future policy, it is apparent that you need to have a deed of gift or deposit agreement that includes clear instructions as to the method of disposition of any items that the historical society does not want.

DESCRIPTION

Case Twenty-One
Karen Benedict, Contributor

You are a project archivist hired by the Sagamore County Historical Society. You job is to create a finding aid for a collection of papers from the U.S. Army Corps of Engineers. The recently honorably discharged major of this unit is a prominent citizen in the town. He has collected the personal papers of the men under his command to document the unit's work on the construction of a dam in Nicaragua. Most of the men in his unit remain close friends and have formed a club called "Bill's Boys" after the major. The project that they worked on became controversial a year ago when the dam collapsed during an earthquake, flooded a village, and killed several hundred people.

These men have donated the letters, photographs, diaries, and other papers in their possession to the major to create what he calls "an archive of the project" to defend his reputation and the quality of the unit's work on the dam and to deny any culpability in the deaths of the Nicaraguan villagers. Despite extensive negative news coverage of this incident, the army did not judge the major and his men as responsible for the accident. It determined that there were no grounds for a court martial or reprimand. Public opinion in the U.S. and in Nicaragua was divided as to their culpability.

The major contacted the director of the historical society to ask if it was interested in the collection. The director, a former military historian, said yes, and informed the chief archivist that he would personally handle the donation agreement.

The director was eager to acquire a collection of so much interest. The major offered to provide funds to process the collection in a calendar year to make it available for research as quickly as possible. The director agreed and said that the historical society would use the money to hire a project archivist whose time would be spent solely in working on this collection to meet the deadline. The director allowed the major to have his attorney amend the donor contract to give the major final approval on all aspects of the project. The chief archivist was presented with the terms of the agreement only after it was signed.

After one month, the major comes to review your initial processing work on the collection. He reads over the descriptive finding aid you are producing while processing the items. He is obviously upset, but says nothing to you. He goes to the chief archivist and says that the work you have done is unsatisfactory and does not meet army standards. He demands to bring in someone from his unit to make corrections and supervise you for the rest of the project. The chief archivist already has reviewed your work and found that it meets archival standards. She has no complaints about your professionalism or the quality of your work. However, the major reminds the chief archivist that he has a right to set his own standards by the terms of the donor agreement. He insists that the chief archivist accede to his request. When the chief archivist tries to reason with him and to calm him, he storms out of the office and goes straight to the director.

A week passes and you hear nothing about changing your work pattern. You continue to process the collection as you have been doing. In the meantime, the chief archivist and director hold several meetings to try to resolve this problem. The chief archivist strongly objects to the major bringing in an unqualified person to supervise your work. She objects to having an unqualified donor dictate how to process a collection. Ultimately, the director says that those are the terms of the donor agreement, and the historical society must abide by them. The chief archivist refuses to cooperate and quits on the spot. The director comes to you and announces that you now are reporting to him. He says it will be necessary to redo all of your work in the manner specified by the major's selected representative. You need the job. The money is paying for your college loans. You also need a good recommendation because this is you first professional position. So, you agree to do as instructed. A corporal is assigned to supervise the project. He has the final say on the descriptive terms you use and the layout of the finding aid. You complete the project, but the level and nature of description is bizarre and does not meet archival professional standards. By the end, you realize that you can never provide a copy of this finding aid as a part of your credentials for another job. In fact, if anyone sees it they probably will not hire you. The chief archivist has not been silent about the reason for her resignation. She has told many of her professional friends about her experience, and she has agreed to do a session on ethics based on her experience at the upcoming annual meeting of SAA.

What should the historical society director have done?

Did the chief archivist behave properly?

What lessons have you, as project archivist, learned from the experience?

The historical society director should not have intervened in creating the donor agreement. He should have let the chief archivist, as a trained professional, negotiate with the major for the donation. He should not have taken the collection if it meant compromising professional standards. Once he signed the donor agreement, the historical society had to honor its terms.

The chief archivist obeyed her conscience. If she stayed on the job, she would violate professional standards and compromise her ethics. On the other hand, without an established career and the likely prospect of finding another job it would be a difficult decision to quit. She might have chosen to stay on and tried to intervene to keep the project on as professional a level as possible. She left a young and inexperienced archivist on his own to deal with a very difficult situation.

The project archivist learned the hard way that an institution's collection policy, its relations with donors, and its procedures for donor and deposit agreements are critical. If an institution does not follow best practice and accepted professional and ethical standards, it will find itself facing serious problems that will damage its reputation and future ability to acquire collections.

DONOR RELATIONS

Case Twenty-Two
Karen Benedict, Contributor

You are the archivist responsible for collections development at the Sagamore County Historical Society. It is your responsibility to seek out donors and purchase collections. You are interested in the papers of Ellsworth Conley, an author from Darby in Sagamore County. Mr. Conley has an international reputation. He left Darby for New York City and ultimately settled in London. His fiction has won many prizes in the U.S. and United Kingdom.

Last year Mr. Conley was back in Darby to visit his mother. The town held a celebration for his homecoming. You were at the reception for him and had an opportunity to talk with him briefly about his papers. Much to your surprise, when he returned to London he wrote to you to indicate an interest in donating his papers to the historical society in recognition of the contribution made by his parents and other family members to his ultimate success as an author.

The director of the historical society is excited at the prospect of the institution getting the papers of such a major figure. The collection will draw scholars and other researchers from all over the world.

When you call Mr. Conley to respond to his letter, he indicates he has had some second thoughts. His agent and his attorney both have suggested to him that he should sell his manuscripts and papers rather than giving them away. You are dismayed by this message because it is obvious that the Sagamore County Historical Society will be at a disadvantage against other more wealthy institutions in competitive bidding for this collection.

However, without discussing explicit terms, you indicate that the historical society is still very interested in his papers. You are unwilling to give up on this acquisition without discussing the possibilities fully with your director and the board. Mr. Conley is delighted to learn that the historical society is willing to negotiate with his representatives.

You notify the director about the present situation and agree to address the board about the collection at its next meeting in a few days.

Before the board meets, Mr. Conley's mother dies unexpectedly of a heart attack. The author returns to Darby for her funeral. Obviously devastated by her sudden death, when he returns home he makes an impulsive decision to place his papers at the historical society in honor of his mother's memory. Conley wastes no time in sending the historical society sixty-five records storage boxes of his papers and manuscripts of his books along with a letter about his wishes. He even doesn't take the time to call you first. You find out when the boxes arrive on your doorstep.

You deliver the good news to the board and the director. They all are elated. You do not have a signed a formal donor agreement with Conley yet, only the letter accompanying the collection. However, you have spoken with him about the necessity of signing a deed of gift to make the legal transfer of ownership to the Sagamore County Historical Society. He has agreed verbally to do so, but said that he was leaving in the morning on a European speaking tour. He will have to handle it upon his return. While in Italy he has a fatal car crash. The attorney for his estate calls and requests the return of all of his materials.

What do you do?

Although you are certain that Mr. Conley meant to follow through with the donor agreement to the historical society, you only have the letter about his wishes that came with the papers to prove it. You think that the sending of the boxes of papers and the letter clearly show his intent. You notify the lawyer about the letter you have. You know that in law, verbal contracts are binding and you mention this fact as well.

The lawyer responds that he is executor of the estate. It is his responsibility to see that the terms of Conley's will are met. The will does not directly mention the disposition of his papers, but they represent a potentially significant part of his monetary worth. He says that if the historical society does not return the papers immediately, he will see you in court.

You must inform the director and the board about this further complication in obtaining the collection. It will be up to them to decide if the historical society is willing to pay legal counsel for advice to see if they should pursue the case, plus lawyer's fees and costs for filing.

You are forced to defend yourself from criticism about your handling of the deed of gift. You respond that the timing was such that if you sent a copy of the deed of gift off to him as soon as you received the boxes, it would not have arrived before his departure for Europe. You feel that you have a good chance of winning in court, but will it be worth it? There will be a lot of publicity. If the outcome is against you, it will hurt the institution's reputation. If you win, on the other hand, you will have made the public aware of the historical society's existence and the kinds of material that it makes available for research. You persuade the director and board to defend the aquisition of these papers.

EQUAL ACCESS AND EQUAL TREATMENT OF USERS

Case Twenty-Three
Timothy Ericson, Contributor

Your "favorite" patron just walked through the door! He comes in once a week and looks through your collection of historical plat maps to locate the site of former farmsteads, town halls, stagecoach stopping places, post offices, schools, and other historical features. Once he finds these sites, he goes there with his metal detector and searches for artifacts that he then sells at flea markets.

You don't really know much about how he goes about his business, but he seems a bit "shady" to you. When you asked him, for example, whether he asks the permission of the current property owners, he gives you evasive answers. He is, however, quite open about some of the valuable artifacts he has found during his "explorations" (his term).

You just received a collection of new nineteenth-century maps that show, among other features, the sites of several previously unknown Indian burial mounds. The maps are not in very good condition and will require some conservation work before they can be made available for use.

As he comes in the door, your "favorite" patron casually mentions that he has just about finished looking through all your maps and asks whether you have anything that he hasn't seen.

How will you respond to him?

What policies will you develop about access to these new acquisitions?

Until the maps have been conserved, they will not be made available for research to anyone. You are justified in telling him that nothing new is open for research.

If these maps are rare, fragile, and of particular historical value, you may want to consider restricting access to them only for serious scholarship. Obviously, previously unknown Indian burial mounds will be of interest to archaeologists, the National Historic Preservation community, the state's division responsible for management of historical sites, and Native American groups. Once the maps are restored, you will want to have a press conference announcing their existence and value for serious research on the early Native American community. All of the publicity and the actions taken by the various agencies involved will focus enough attention on the sites to discourage the casual fortune seeker.

Case Twenty-Four
Karen Benedict, Contributor

You are an archivist working in the Center for American History at Sagamore State University. The center holds the papers of many local and state politicians. Ten years ago, state senator Robert Puckle deposited his papers at the center. Puckle was the champion of the state's Open Records Act, which provided the public with access to all public records.

Puckle's collection is a mix of personal papers and records relating to his career in the state legislature. The deposit agreement states that the papers will become the center's property at the end of Puckle's active political career. In the meantime, the papers are restricted access, open to university faculty and students for educational purposes only.

Puckle is now the Democratic candidate for U.S. Congress in the university's congressional district. The campaign manager for his Republican opponent has applied for access to the papers under the Open Records Act. The center director tells you to notify Puckle immediately of the request for access. Puckle responds by stating that these are his personal papers not subject to the Open Records Act. He threatens to take back his papers from the center before he will allow them to be made available to his opponent.

"They are my papers," Puckle states. "I loaned them to the university for legitimate educational research purposes. I am not obligated to assist my political opponent in his search for information that he and his people can use to attack me during the campaign. This is not a legitimate research request."

The center director tells you not to allow the campaign manager to see the records because of the restrictions. The campaign manager arrives at your office accompanied by members of the press. He says that the records relate to Puckle's time in the state legislature. He should have access to them because Puckle and his staff created them while he was serving as state senator.

What are the institution's legal and ethical responsibilities in this case?

What do you in regard to the access issue?

The center has a signed deposit agreement with state senator Puckle. Under the agreement, access is limited to university faculty and students for educational purposes only. The center must abide by the terms of the agreement; it does not own the documents and cannot arbitrarily change the restrictions on access. The papers are still Puckle's property. If the campaign manager wishes to pursue access under the state's Open Records Act, the legal action is against Puckle not the center. You deny access and explain the above reasons to the campaign manager and his press entourage. You prepare a public statement to this effect, in case they do decide to pursue the matter.

Case Twenty-Five
Karen Benedict, Contributor

You are the new chief archivist for the Whitney Falls Athenaeum and Historical Society in Sagamore Falls. It is a well-endowed private historical society that has an excellent collection of colonial period manuscripts, private papers, and records.

Located in the same town is the Wiscasset House, the home of the first governor of the colony. Wiscasset House is owned and administered by a local private, nonprofit association. The house is open for tours of its period-furnished rooms, and it maintains an archives of the governor's private papers and the earliest town records dating from the 1740s to the 1790s. Volunteers from the community staff it.

You have been elected to serve on the board of governors of Wiscasset House. Your boss, the director of the historical society, is delighted because it provides you with an opportunity to work with some of the leading citizens in town. The historical society is launching a large fund-raising campaign to remodel its building and to increase storage space for the collection. The director hopes that your work with Wiscasset House will make important connections that will help in this effort.

You are the first professional archivist to serve on the Wiscasset House board. The board and staff are both eager and apprehensive about your input and evaluation of how they are doing.

In preparation for your first board meeting you have been looking into the operations of Wiscasset House. The volunteer staff consists entirely of financial supporters from the community. It is considered prestigious to be selected by the board to serve as a volunteer there.

Although you were aware that the staff was not professionally trained, subsequently you have discovered that the rules governing procedures are unorthodox and do not conform to accepted professional standards. Moreover, there are no printed guides or finding aids to the collections. Researchers at

Wiscasset House are forced to rely on an incomplete and unreliable card catalog of subjects and the knowledge and assistance of the volunteer staff to locate materials for their research projects. Your staff has alerted you to rumors that the volunteers routinely deny records access to people they dislike or for projects of which they disapprove. Allegedly, the volunteer staff frequently prevents researchers from seeing all of the available papers in a collection.

You are concerned already about how to broach discussion of the problems at Wiscasset House, when a researcher at your repository asks to speak with you about a problem that she has had there. The researcher has just learned that you are a new appointee to the board, which is to meet at the end of the week. She relates to you her recent experience at Wiscasset House and asks your opinion as to whether the staff's conduct was unethical or unprofessional.

She says that two weeks ago she was doing research there in town records for the book she is writing on colonial township administration. She observed that a volunteer removed papers from several folders before delivering them to her, and then denied that she had done so when the researcher questioned her.

The researcher has prepared a written statement of the events, naming the volunteer involved. She asks you to present this at the next board meeting. She says that she is considering making a formal complaint against Wiscasset House through the Society of American Archivists and the American Historical Association.

The volunteer named in the researcher's complaint is the wife of one of the members of the Wiscasset House board, a prominent businessman in the community. The director of the historical society has told you he would like to name this gentleman as chairman of the society's fund-raising campaign.

What are your ethical and legal obligations to your employer and to Wiscasset House?

How will you handle the researcher's complaint?

You have an obligation to go to your director and inform him about the complaint you have received from the researcher. You also need to tell him about your findings in regard to the procedures and operations of Wiscasset House.

As a professional archivist and a member of the board of governors of Wiscasset House you will need to address the irregularities in the operations there. You should put your remarks into a written report that is well balanced between emphasizing the value of the collections and their importance to the research community and discussing the need to improve Wiscasset House's procedures and services. You need to be constructive not destructive in your criticisms, but you are obligated to give the board an honest professional appraisal.

As for the researcher's complaint, you should make copies for all the board members with a brief cover letter explaining how you came to be the recipient of it. The board of governors as a whole will have to determine how it will address the issue. You can suggest that it give the researcher an opportunity to come and speak to the board directly. That will give the governors a chance to evaluate the complaint, question the complainant, and respond to her directly. If they are able to satisfy her through an examination of the facts and a response about the way in which they will deal with the situation, it is possible that she will not feel it necessary to pursue the issue with outside bodies.

It is not an enviable task, but having accepted the position it is your duty to do the best professional job possible.

INFORMATION ABOUT RESEARCHERS

Case Twenty-Six
Karen Benedict, Contributor

You are the archivist for Bellevue University located in the southwestern corner of the county. A liberal arts college with a strong national reputation in American literature, Bellevue's archives has the papers of a number of well-known novelists and poets, many of whom are or were members of the faculty. Two Pulitzer Prize winners are alumni of the college. One of the Pulitzer winners is a poet known for his left wing politics as well as his poetry. The poet is of Arab parentage, although born in the United States. After 9/11, he is an outspoken critic of the U.S. government's alleged persecution of Arab Americans and of the U.S. policy vis-á-vis Israel. Some of his recent poetry contains imagery that is violent and could be interpreted as anti-Semitic, although it is not explicit in content.

Users who want to see the poet's recent papers besiege the archives. A local synagogue is defaced, and when the culprits are found to be two Arab American students from the university, the national press surmises that the poet and his writings influenced the students. Several reporters come to the archives to see the poet's papers and to find out whether those two students looked at his papers recently. You protest that the information about users is confidential. The newspapers view your refusal as evidence that you are protecting the poet and the students, and it becomes a major story in the national news. The university's president is quite upset by the bad publicity. You are summoned by the president to explain your reasons for not disclosing the information on use of the materials to the press. The president doesn't seem to listen to your explanation and demands that you cooperate with the press.

What do you do?

Although the "Code of Ethics" does not directly address this issue, Section IX states that "Archivists do not reveal the details of one researcher's work to others. . . . Archivists also are sensitive to the needs of confidential research. . . ." The American Library Association has a more pertinent stand that it will not reveal any information about its users because that violates their privacy.

It would be best if you could directly refer to the archivists "Code of Ethics" as a source for your stand not to reveal this information to the press. In lieu of that, you can make the parallel case with the ALA and say that you are unwilling on ethical grounds to release this information to the press. Morally, you should take the high ground and refuse to violate the privacy of your donors or your users.

INSTITUTIONAL BEST PRACTICES

Case Twenty-Seven
Timothy Ericson, Contributor

The Sagamore Regional Archives Center (SRAC) where you work has just uncovered the theft of several very valuable Civil War letters. There is a good deal of suspicion that the theft was an inside job committed by a former staff member (a Civil War enthusiast and collector). He was fired two years ago after the repeated discovery of Civil War records in his desk drawer and his briefcase. He claimed that he was using the records for "research."

By a stroke of luck, most of the missing letters were photocopied as a part of a recent project, so a large percentage of the information has been preserved.

You have absolutely no proof that the former staff member stole the materials. Under the circumstances, the SRAC director feels very strongly that it would be just as well not to report the theft to the local police. She says it would likely result in bad publicity for SRAC and would reflect poorly on the institution's security procedures and integrity. More to the point, news of a theft might adversely affect the completion of a large donation of materials that are scheduled to be given by the same donor who gave the Civil War letters.

Is it legal and/or ethical to suppress information about the theft?

What is the responsibility of the administration to the potential donor and to the institution in the aftermath of this incident?

Section VI in the "Code of Ethics for Archivists" states, "Archivists protect the integrity of documentary materials of long-term value in their custody, guarding them against defacement, alteration, theft, and physical damage. . . . They cooperate with other archivists and law enforcement agencies in the apprehension and prosecution of thieves."

Despite the embarrassment factor, it is not ethical to suppress information about a theft at your institution. You are obliged to protect and to attempt to recover material that is a part of your collections. You jeopardize the integrity and security of other institutions by not actively working to apprehend and prosecute individuals who steal from archives.

Your potential donor will not be impressed by a refusal to do your utmost to retrieve materials taken from your archives and to prosecute the perpetrators of the crime. You must use any theft as a lesson in the limitations of your present security system and work to improve security and eliminate risk.

OWNERSHIP OF RECORDS

Case Twenty-Eight
Timothy Ericson, Contributor

You are university archivist at Sagamore State University. The widow of a former university president has asked you to look over some of her late husband's papers—he had died suddenly in office back in the early 1960s, and his papers were packed up by his former secretary. No archives existed at the time. The papers were placed in storage, and this is your first opportunity to appraise the material. As you look over the collection (approximately five cubic feet of material), it becomes clear to you that this material comprises not his "personal papers" but official university records that never should have been taken from the president's office.

Among the files you notice one that relates to the resignation of a former faculty member in 1958. The faculty member, also deceased, was very popular on campus—you have heard his name many times. In fact, the faculty senate recently proposed naming a building in his honor. He had been a good friend of the late president, and his sudden departure was a mystery to everyone on campus. However, the file makes it clear that he was forced to resign because of a questionable personal relationship with an undergraduate student.

The late president's wife is aware of the file's contents and is uncomfortable about turning it over to you. She has indicated that she may destroy this file before handing over the other papers.

How do you deal with the widow's concerns?

What action do you take if she does destroy the file that is university property?

Are there issues that you need to resolve with your administration?

You should explain to the president's wife that these files are not the president's personal property, but are the official files of his term as president of the university. There was not an archives, of course, when he retired, but these records are legitimately the property of the university and should be in the archives. You also should reassure her that the archives is aware that files may contain sensitive information and has a policy to restrict access to such information for a reasonable length of time. While both the president and former professor are dead, the student mentioned in the case likely is still alive. So, you would restrict access to this file until her death is verified or for a reasonable period of time, perhaps thirty years.

Beyond the notification before the fact that she would be destroying university property, it would be difficult to take any action against the widow if she went ahead and carried out the action. In addition to bad publicity for the archives, making the case public would require divulging some information about the file that was destroyed. Even if names were suppressed, a discussion of aspects of the case probably would allow some individuals to surmise the identity of the professor in question.

If the archives does not have a policy in place stating that the official records of the president are the property of the university and belong in the archives after the president's term is completed, then you should make the administration aware of the need for such a policy. The university's president needs to know that this is the proper disposition for his files in the future. You may need to seek out the papers of other university presidents whose tenure ended before the establishment of the archives.

PRIVACY

Case Twenty-Nine
Timothy Ericson, Contributor

You are processing a collection of personal papers that belonged to the daughter of a locally prominent family. The daughter was a nationally successful author who was just on the verge of achieving international prominence when her personal life took a disastrous turn in a nasty divorce. A short time later she was killed in a car accident that some allege was a suicide.

Her parents took their daughter's death very hard because she was their only child. Now, after almost ten years, they finally have been convinced to donate her papers to your archives so that they can be available for research. The papers are an unrestricted gift. The parents are very old and in poor health. They spend most of their time at their Florida home.

As you are processing the papers, you come across an envelope containing a series of photographs. They are not at all pornographic, but they clearly demonstrate a relationship between the author and the man with her. Nothing has been written that even hinted at her having an extramarital affair. However, these photographs have notes on the back indicating that the two were more than friends. You do not know the identity of the man in the photographs, but wonder whether these pictures shed some light on the events surrounding the divorce and subsequent car accident.

Clearly the writer's parents did not know that these photographs were included with their donation of their daughter's papers. You are concerned about the reaction of the parents if they become aware of the existence of these photographs and their implications. The wife has recently had a major heart attack and the husband also has heart problems.

Would you keep the photographs in the collection? Return them? Or destroy them?

If you kept them, would you restrict access to them?

Do you bear any responsibility for the health consequences to the parents if a revelation of the photos' existence adversely affects them?

Destroying the photographs would be destroying a part of the evidentiary record of the author's life. You would alter that record if you returned the photographs to her parents. So, you decide to keep the photographs in the collection. You will restrict access to them for a length of time until it is reasonable to expect that the man pictured is dead, thus maintaining his right to privacy. The man appears to be in his mid- to late thirties. You will restrict access for fifty years.

The collection was an unrestricted gift to the archives, and you would have no legal liability if information about the photographs' existence adversely affected the health of the writer's aged parents. However, as a matter of personal conscience and morality, you should make every effort to maintain the privacy of this information and not allow it to harm her parents or their memory of their daughter.

Case Thirty
Mark Greene, Contributor

You are the curator of manuscripts for Sagamore State Historical Society. Three years ago, you were approached by an elderly gentleman living outside the city of Riverfield who had some family papers he wanted to donate. You visited him and found about a cubic foot of papers from three generations of his family, 1840–1950. The papers included courtship letters and poetry; diaries of his grandmother, Rachel, a rural schoolteacher (1889–1894); diaries of his mother, Helen, a rural housewife (1896–1905); and correspondence, much of it exchanged among his five siblings (Rebecca, Clarissa, Mary, John, and William) and their parents (Helen and Charles). Closer examination revealed that virtually all the letters were sent to Rebecca or to her mother, except for a handful of letters from the donor, James, to Clarissa and William.

James explained that it was via his mother, Helen, that he had inherited the papers. Before she died, she gave the papers to his sister, Clarissa, who passed them on to her brother. He further explained that his brother John was a "black sheep" who, after a ne'er-do-well existence, had committed suicide. His troubles and the concern that he caused the family were well documented in the papers (which even include his suicide note).

You carefully explained to the donor that he could specify in the deed of gift that some of the papers could be restricted, if he wished to delay public access to the tragic side of his family's history. He responded, however, that as only he and his elder brother William, who was ninety-four, were still alive, this was not necessary. He had read every letter himself and he was perfectly content to have all the papers publicly accessible from the start. As it was an excellent family collection, for a relatively under-documented portion of the state, you gladly accepted the papers and an unrestricted deed of gift.

This morning, without warning, a woman appears in your office and identifies herself as Clarissa's daughter. She has just learned that her uncle donated the family papers and is furious that this was done without her consent. She did not want all this material made public and objects to her family's "dirty laundry" being available for just anyone to read. She asks you to give the entire collection to her. You politely explain that her uncle attested to his ownership of the papers and his right to donate them. The historical society will not surrender them to her.

In response, she argues that she has a right to control disposition of at least the material written by or about her mother, Clarissa. She then demands that any letters written by or to Clarissa be returned to her.

What is your response?

What if instead she had insisted that Clarissa's papers have access restricted?

Since she is her descendent, what would be your response?

She did not donate the papers, and the archives cannot give them to her. If she wants to contest their ownership, that is an issue that she must take up with her Uncle James.

If she had asked for Clarissa's paper to be restricted because she is her daughter, she should be made aware that privacy rights die with the individual. However, you could have offered to go through the letters to and from Clarissa with her to see if any of the information in them was sensitive. If any embarrassing disclosures or denigrating information about individuals are mentioned in the letters, you could agree to restrict those letters for a reasonable length of time. You would need to notify the donor, James, of your decision and tell him that you also will apply the same restrictions to other letters on the same basis.

Case Thirty-One
Robert Spindler, Contributor

You are the archivist at Sagamore State University where the archives holds the records of the South Central Survey Research Laboratory (SCSRL). The laboratory is an office of the university that conducts surveys funded by the public and private sector. Last month, the SCSRL conducted a telephone survey of county residents to determine mobility patterns for traffic control and highway construction planning.

The data collected includes preferred method, direction, and duration of travel from home to office; household income information; and names, addresses, and telephone numbers of individual respondents. Telephone interviewers were instructed to inform interviewees about the purpose of the survey and to promise their responses would be confidential. Since SCSRL studies have been identified as archival, SCSRL deposits its data in the university archives soon after they are created. Often the two offices work together to make the raw data public in support of SCSRL projects.

To support public meetings concerning highway planning, the archives and SCSRL mounted portions of the data on the archives Web site—omitting all personal identifiers and household income to protect the privacy of the interviewees.

A few days after the data are mounted on the Web site, an executive officer of Sellitnow Marketing contacts you. He suggests that the archives has illegally destroyed the public record by removing the personally identifiable information. He demands a reproduction of the entire raw data set, which he intends to sell as a marketing research tool.

Do you provide him with the data?

What are the legal, ethical, and privacy issues involved?

No, you do not provide Sellitnow Marketing with the data. You tell the executive that the data are the legal property of SCSRL and are deposited for safekeeping, security, and confidentiality in the university archives. You also tell the executive officer that the data set contains confidential information. SCSRL has an agreement with all respondents that their privacy will be protected. It would be unethical for you to provide him with the original data. The public record has not been destroyed by the elimination of personal identifiers. The original data set is maintained in the archives. The aggregate data that have been placed on the Web site are available for researchers because they do not contain confidential information.

Case Thirty-Two
Robert Sink, Contributor

You are on the reference desk of the Sagamore County Historical Society when a patron (and large contributor to the operating fund) comes up to you carrying a letter from one of your collections.

The patron is extremely angry and thrusts the letter in your face. "I want this destroyed immediately," the patron fumes.

You try to calm the situation by asking what the problem is.

"This letter is full of lies," is the response. After additional questioning, the patron says that the letter writer asserts that the patron's grandfather was a drunk and that this is obviously false because his grandfather was a staunch member of the local Baptist church all of his life.

What are your legal and ethical recourses to deal with the patron's complaint?

Should you take any action, even if you could do so?

You explain to the patron that you understand fully why this letter is upsetting to him, but you cannot destroy material in the archives. It would be unethical to do so. You then have a choice to make. You can tell the patron that you will look into the matter to see if you have any recourse in dealing with this letter. Or you can explain that his grandfather's right to privacy under law ceased when he died. Although this letter is offensive to the patron, it is the responsibility of the researcher to look at the facts and evaluate its credibility. If you choose to look at options for dealing with the letter to satisfy the patron, then you must do so in a professional manner. You can carefully read the letter to see if it contains other information that has historical or evidentiary signif-icance. You should also evaluate the significance of the letter in the context of the collection it comes from to see whether or not it lends contextual value that would be harmed if access to the letter were restricted for a reasonable period of time. You will need to check the donor agreement to see if there are any special provisions regarding restricting access to items in the collection. Should no valid reason to restrict access exist, you can place a limited restric-tion on access to the letter to respond to the patron's sensitivity about his grandfather's reputation.

PROFESSIONAL ACTIVITIES

Case Thirty-Three
Karen Benedict, Contributor

You are the archivist at Slippery Elm State College. Your institution has made a major advance from a junior college to a four-year institution. Even as a junior college, the administration supported the archives and maintained an adequate budget for staff and services. However, travel funds have never been available to the archives staff members.

Now with the advance to a degree-conferring institution, you are hoping that you can get support for professional activities. You approach your super-visor with a request to join the Society of American Archivists and to attend the annual meeting. You show your supervisor a program for the upcoming meeting in which you have underlined the sessions and workshops of particular interest to you. While your supervisor agrees that participation would be a good thing for you, she says that she cannot justify paying your travel expenses when other employees in the library and archives do not receive travel funds. The institu-tion only gives travel support when the staff member is presenting a paper, participating on a panel, giving a workshop, or chairing a session at the conference of the association. She says that she is willing to have you take the time off as paid leave, but that you will need to pay your own travel and costs as others do who attend meetings of the American Library Association.

Your pay scale is less than that of the senior librarians who attend ALA meetings. However, you know that you will need to attend professional meet-ings and publish articles if you want to move up the career ladder and/or seek another professional position somewhere else.

Is it your responsibility to make the sacrifice and pay your own costs for professional activities?

The commentary on Section XII, Professional Activities, says, "Archivists may choose to join or not to join local, state, regional, and national professional organizations, but they must be well-informed about changes in archival functions and they must have some contact with their colleagues. They should share their expertise by participation in professional meetings and by publishing. By such activities, in the field of archives, in related fields, and in their own special interests, they continue to grow professionally."

Nothing compels archivists to join professional associations except their own desire for regular connection with their colleagues and the opportunity to keep abreast of new developments in the profession. The meetings also provide the chance for continuing education and training in many areas.

In this case, you have some choices. If you want to improve your credentials and continue to learn more about the field, it is important to join a professional association and attend meetings whenever possible. Joining SAA or MAC will provide you with a regular newsletter and a journal of timely articles in the field. At least you will receive your regular salary while at the meeting, which will help to defray some of the costs. The other choice is to participate in a session at the program, in which case the full costs will be covered. Session proposal forms are available on the SAA Web site and the ArchivesList often has calls for participants to round out a program suggestion. It will take some effort on your part, but it can be done. The rewards of participation should eventually make a difference in your qualifications and salary scale.

PROFESSIONAL CONDUCT AND PERSONAL PROFIT FROM WORK

Case Thirty-Four
Karen Benedict, Contributor

You have just gotten your first professional position as a project archivist at the Sagamore County Historical Society (SCHS). It is a grant-funded position to assist in the processing of the congressional papers, and personal papers relating to his time in Congress, of a former U.S. congressman from the SCHS's district. He is now vice president of the United States.

You are assisting an experienced archivist in processing the papers. This archivist will give you a performance evaluation that will be used to help determine whether or not to offer you a permanent position with SCHS at the end of the project period.

While working with the archivist, you note that she is removing stamped envelopes from correspondence in the collection and putting them aside. The congressman did not use his franking privilege for most of his correspondence. You follow her example, and at the end of the day she adds your pile to her own. At the end of the week, you see her put this pile of envelopes into her briefcase. She presumably takes them home with her at the end of the workday on Friday.

You are puzzled by her actions and decide to ask her about what she does with the envelopes on Monday morning. When you question her about this on Monday, she is clearly upset and angry. She tells you that she has a young son who is a stamp collector and she gives him the stamps that would otherwise be thrown away.

You are not entirely satisfied with the explanation. You wonder if what she is doing may be unethical. You screw up your courage and go to speak to the head archivist about this practice. However, at the last moment you decide not to "tell" on the archivist. Instead, you pose a question about the institution's policies and procedures regarding stamped envelopes with correspondence in collections.

The head archivist says that it is the policy to remove stamped envelopes from the collections. Ordinary stamps are discarded and those with potential value are evaluated for possible sale to benefit SCHS.

No further mention is made of the incident, but the archivist is noticeably cooler and more critical in her dealings with you. You try to make amends because you hope to get a good performance evaluation from her. In your last two months of the project, you feel that you have repaired your relationship with her.

On the weekend before your last week of project work and your scheduled performance evaluation, you are in the local mall and notice a display of stamp collections and stamps for sale by the local Boy Scout troop. You stroll by and see the archivist and her son at a table with stamps displayed for sale. Several of the envelopes are personal letters from the congressman. You recognize his handwriting and his return address. The stamps are not of special significance, but the vice president's handwriting is a selling point.

The archivist bristles when she sees you looking at the envelopes. She defends their sale by saying that they were just going to be thrown away by SCHS and that the money will go to benefit the local Boy Scout troop. You try to act casual and say that it is a pleasant surprise to run into her with her son, and you leave as soon as you can without appearing to run away.

Do you have an ethical obligation to do something in a case like this?

What will you do knowing that your actions have an impact on your performance review and your future career?

You can tell by the archivist's reaction to the situation that she is not comfortable with her actions. You realize that you are in a bad situation and will need to address it in some way on Monday. At home, you go to the SAA Web page and look for the "Code of Ethics" to guide you. You read through it and find nothing that is completely on point. The archivist shouldn't steal from the archives, but this is not a true case of theft. She has taken items that the SCHS throws away. Technically, this is not a good thing to do, but it is not theft. About profiting from your work the code only says, "[Archivists] neither reveal nor profit from information gained through work with restricted holdings."

That stipulation does not apply to this case either. The archivist has entered a gray area. You debate with yourself and conclude that she and her son are not personally profiting from this if the money goes to support the Boy Scout troop. You decide that it is probably unprofessional for the archivist to take the envelopes and that the best thing to do is to go in and talk with the archivist honestly about the situation on Monday morning. You will tell her your reasoning about whether or not she violated ethics in taking the envelopes. You will leave it to her to decide if she has been unprofessional in her conduct. You hope that you can talk this out in a professional and low-key manner and resolve your conflict with her. If not, and if she lets this incident affect her performance review of your work, then you will have to bring the matter up to the head archivist for her to resolve.

PROTECTION OF INTEGRITY OF DOCUMENTS

Case Thirty-Five
Timothy Ericson, Contributor

The president of the largest campus fraternity comes to the archives. He has a copy of the fraternity's charter—a large, attractive, and expensive document that is on parchment-like paper with a seal and written in calligraphy.

Unfortunately, the ink on the lower half of the document has been badly smeared. The president asks whether you can "fix" the document. The fraternity has a formal event coming up and would like to display the charter—but not in its present state. Among the guests who will be at the upcoming event are several representatives from the national office. The local fraternity was supposed to have the original charter framed, but never got around to doing it.

You ask what caused the document to become smeared. He replies, "Sweat." You don't want to know any more.

A reporter from the campus newspaper is at the archives doing some research and becomes very interested in learning whether this is something with which an archives can help.

The fraternity president leaves the document. Both he and the reporter will stop back in a couple of days. The only way you know to remove the smear is to use an ink eraser pen. It is very abrasive to the paper, but does a fairly good job of removing the smeared ink. The abrasion will hardly be noticeable once the document is encapsulated. You have the time to clean up and encapsulate the document before the formal event they are planning. To do so would be a great public relations coup for your archives.

What will you do?

You contact the president of the fraternity and ask him to meet with you in the archives to discuss his options for restoring the document. When he comes, you explain what you would be capable of doing in time for the planned event. You make sure that he understands that using the ink eraser pen will permanently abrade the paper the document is on, but that you think that encapsulation will hide most of the damage done to the paper's surface. You explain that this will be irreversible damage. His option is to seek out a paper conservator, and you will help him to locate ones that are nearby. The conservator will evaluate the damage and tell the fraternity what can be done and how much it will cost for restoration. This means that the fraternity will have to own up to the damage to the charter and explain that they are in the process of having it professionally restored. You tell him that it is the fraternity's decision what to do, but that you advise that professional restoration would be the best course to follow.

Case Thirty-Six
Leon Miller, Contributor

You are the manuscripts archivist at Sagamore-Abington College, a moderately prestigious, midsized private college. One of your department's specialties is preserving the literary heritage of the region. Your most prized collection is the papers of Robert Bruster, a New York-based literary critic who retired to your area.

Your library also houses a small rare books collection. Perhaps its best know collection is the personal library of Anna Ospenskaya, a major twentieth-century Russian poetess. After working with the Ospenskaya collection for many years, your rare books librarian has become an Ospenskaya buff and constantly searches for Ospenskaya-related items to add to the rare books unit. In addition to purchasing new editions of her works, the rare books unit preserves Ospenskaya commemorative postcards, bookmarks, ashtrays, telephone calling cards, and even a bottle of Ospenskaya vodka.

Robert Bruster was a lifelong friend of Ospenskaya's. They maintained a steady and rich correspondence over more than thirty years, and his papers preserve their complete correspondence: the originals of all of her letters to him as well as copies of his letters to her. Her letters are interfiled by date within the rest of his correspondence. Therefore, the Bruster correspondence comprises a single chronological series. Ospenskaya's letters to Bruster are well known within the research community. They have been heavily used and are the major portion of the Bruster papers' intellectual value.

One day, your rare books librarian goes to your supervisor, the head of special collections, and proposes to remove the Ospenskaya letters from the Bruster papers and add them to the rare books unit's Ospenskaya collection. Your supervisor readily agrees. Neither the rare books librarian nor the head of special collections discusses the matter with you. You learn of the decision when you discover the rare books librarian in your stacks, rummaging through the Bruster papers and removing the Ospenskaya correspondence.

What would your arguments be to the rare books librarian and head of special collections to protest their actions and ask them to return the Ospenskaya correspondence?

What are the alternatives open to you to deal with the transfer of your collection to another archives?

You need to explain to the head of special collections and the rare books librarian that these letters legally are a part of the Robert Bruster collection and are covered in the deed of gift to the archives. They are not to be removed without the permission of Robert Bruster or the archivist. The removal of the letters is a violation of the "Code of Ethics for Archivists." The code states that "[Archivists] maintain and protect the arrangement of documents and information transferred to their custody to protect its authenticity. Archivists protect the integrity of documentary materials of long-term value in their custody, guarding them against defacement, alteration, theft, and physical damage, and ensure that their evidentiary value is not impaired in the archival work of arrangement, description, preservation, and use."

You state that removing the letters of Ospenskaya from the context of the exchange of information between Bruster and Ospenskaya damages their evidentiary value.

You ask for their immediate return. To try to maintain a good working relationship with the head of special collections and the rare books librarian, you suggest that you would be willing to make photocopies of the letters from Ospenskaya for the rare books librarian's collection. However, acknowledgement must be made that the original copies are in the archives with the Bruster correspondence.

RESEARCH BY ARCHIVISTS

Case Thirty-Seven
Karen Benedict, Contributor

You are the manuscripts curator and head of special collections at the Bellevue College Library. You were hired as an assistant professor in the library in a tenure track position. You are required to engage in professional activities and to publish articles and monographs to be promoted and achieve tenure. Your undergraduate degree is in English literature, and you have a master's degree in Library and Information Services. Your research interests are in literature. You decide to write a biography of Margaret Todd, a novelist and nonfiction writer whose papers are in your holdings. No biography of Todd has been done. You know that her papers and diaries provide a rich source of biographical information that would enable you to craft an interesting biography. You secure the permission of the library director to use her papers for your work.

You have worked for two years researching her life and her career on weekends and in your vacation time. You are well prepared to begin your biography. The project is exciting for you, and you have talked with several professors in the English department about your research. One of them happens to mention your project to a friend of his, Amy Semple, a published author and biographer. Ms. Semple expresses amazement at not knowing that Todd's papers were in Bellevue library's special collections. She has long had an interest in Todd's life and would like to write about her. She wastes no time in securing an advance from her publisher for a Todd biography. Before you have had a chance to begin your writing, she arrives at special collections ready to start work on her book. You are dismayed when you interview her about her project. You realize that she already has a publisher and a track record as a writer. She will be working full time on her book and will finish long before you are able to do so.

Should you tell her about your project?

Even though you are the best-informed member of staff to help her with her research, can you decline to do so on the basis of conflict of interest with your own project?

The "Code of Ethics" says, "The fact that archivists are doing research in their institutional archives should be made known to patrons, and archivists should not reserve materials for their own use. Because it increases their familiarity with their own collections, this kind of research should make it possible for archivists to be more helpful to other researchers. Archivists are not obliged, any more than other researchers are, to reveal the details of their work or the fruits of their research."

So, you are obliged to tell her that you are researching Margaret Todd. You do not need to disclose any more details than that to her. She asks if you have published anything yet. You say no, but this gives you an idea. You will use your research to craft an article or two about Margaret Todd. Articles count as publications as well as books for your tenure review. In this way, you can make it clear that your Margaret Todd project precedes Ms. Semple's work. If you want to continue to work on a full biography you can do so, or you can move onto another topic.

You cannot use conflict of interest as a reason not to assist Ms. Semple. Your primary responsibility is as head of special collections and not as author. If you do not want to work directly with Semple and wish to assign another staff member to work with her, you, as expert in the papers, must answer your staff member's questions about the collection. You need to help in any way you are able to see that Semple gets a professional level of service.

RESTRICTIONS ON ACCESS TO DOCUMENTS

Case Thirty-Eight
Robert Sink, Contributor

Sagamore State's manuscript repository acquired the papers of a recently deceased politician. His widow was the donor of the collection, and she signed an unrestricted deed of gift. You promise to provide her with a copy of the finding aid your repository creates for the collection.

During accessioning, a staff member finds confidential personnel memos and letters of recommendation among the papers. You decide that these materials should be closed during the lifetime of the individuals concerned. You notify the widow of your decision as a matter of courtesy.

Later, while processing the correspondence files, a staff member finds two folders of letters exchanged between the politician and his lover in another city. Some of these letters are quite explicit in describing the nature of the relationship. The staff member alerts you to their existence.

What do you do?

You will handle the restriction of these letters in the same way that you handled the other sensitive material in the collection. These materials will be closed during the lifetime of the individuals involved, the lover and the wife. You do have a choice as to whether or not you will notify the wife of the restrictions as you did in the other case. You can choose to tell her that the staff has found additional personal correspondence and is restricting access to it on the same conditions as the other items, without going into further detail. Since the donation was an unrestricted gift, and the manuscript repository has ownership, it is entitled to set reasonable restrictions on access. The restrictions apply to the wife as well as any other researcher. You do not know if the wife was aware of her husband's infidelity or not. You do not want to cause her emotional harm by disclosing his affair if she does not know. Infidelity on the part of politicians is not the shocking revelation it once was in the 1950s and 1960s. We have come to see it as a frequent occurrence and do not judge it as harshly today. Once all the individuals involved are deceased, the knowledge of this affair will not directly harm the reputation of any living individual. If children are involved, you may wish to consider their interests and sensitivities as well.

THEFT

Case Thirty-Nine
Karen Benedict, Contributor

You work in the special collections department of Dean Library at Sagamore-Ruthven College, a private liberal arts college. The library received a substantial endowment from Eliazar Ruthven, a self-made millionaire from Sagamore. Some of the endowment was used, as per his bequest, to purchase literary manuscripts and papers of midwestern authors. The special collections department is well known for its extensive holdings of American manuscripts.

Over the past three years, special collections has discovered that a number of signed letters by several famous authors are missing. The curator of special collections feels that all of these thefts were the work of a single individual. His suspicions are focused on a particular professor of American literature from Indiana. He has been a frequent visitor to special collections and is the only patron to have used all of the collections from which letters are missing.

The library has experienced cutbacks and only two staff members are left in special collections, you and the curator. There is no longer sufficient staff to handle security and to keep an eye on users in the reading room at all times. Moreover, the cutbacks have meant that the library has eliminated the guards who used to search patrons' book bags and briefcases when they entered and exited the library.

It is spring break, and the Indiana professor has returned to use other literary collections. The curator has told you to bring only one box at a time for the professor to use and to allow him to look only at materials in a single folder at a time. You are instructed to carefully check the contents of each folder against the box/folder inventory before and after use by the professor.

The professor is upset by the delays this causes in receiving and returning materials for his research. He protests the slow service because his research time is limited. He demands to have access to entire boxes at once. You tell him that this is a new policy and that you cannot waive it for him. He asks to speak to the curator.

The curator reiterates what you have said and refuses to make an exception in his case. The professor then goes to the director of the library and protests his treatment. The director calls in the curator and asks why he was not informed of this change in policy. The curator has told the director about the missing items, but not about his suspicions as to the identity of the culprit. He tries to explain to the director that he feels it necessary to take these precautions with this particular patron. The director reprimands the curator for singling out the professor and restricting his access to materials without any proof of wrongdoing on his part. He tells the curator to allow the professor the same access as other users of special collections have always had in the past, but to come back to him if and when there is evidence that the professor is stealing materials.

The curator agrees to abide by the director's instructions. He tells you that you will handle the change by only carefully checking the contents of each box the professor returns against the box/folder inventories. He also instructs you to sit across the table from the professor and to keep an eye on him the entire time he is doing his research.

You are given some photographs to sort while sitting at the reading room table. It makes you very uncomfortable to pretend to work while watching the professor. You can tell that he resents your presence.

Another difficulty is that the special collections reading room does not close over the lunch hour. Arrangements must be made for someone to cover for you while you're on your lunch break. A graduate student, who normally works at the circulation desk, is commandeered to fill in for you.

At the end of the fourth day, you are checking through the boxes the professor has used, and you find an empty folder. You tell the curator, and he is terribly upset, asking whether you watched the professor closely while you were on duty. You respond that you did and that you did not observe the professor stealing any papers from any folders. The graduate student also swears that he did not see anything unusual either.

Not having checked the box before the professor used the material means that you do not have concrete evidence that the papers were there in the folder when he received the box. However, he has been the only patron to use this collection since it was processed.

What do you do?

The curator goes to the library director and explains what has occurred. The curator wants to confront the professor, but the library director prefers a less aggressive approach.

The next morning the curator and the professor are asked to come to the director's office. The director tells the professor that one of the folders in a box he used yesterday is empty. The professor says that he noticed that it was empty when he went through the material in the box. The curator asks him why he did not bring that fact to his attention or to the attention of his assistant. The professor said he found it over the assistant's lunch hour and planned to tell her when she returned from lunch. But he got immersed in work and it entirely slipped his mind.

The curator is upset by the professor's cavalier attitude to the missing material. He mentions that this is not the first time that material has been discovered to be missing after the professor used a collection. The professor remains calm and says that he has never taken any items from the collections here. The library director asks the curator if there is any proof of his accusation. The curator replies that it must be more than a coincidence that the professor has been here working on four occasions, and material is missing from each of the collections he has used. However, this does not constitute proof. The professor says that since he clearly is not welcome, he will leave today.

The curator and director continue to discuss the problem. The curator says that it is their obligation to call the police and report the theft of material. The director is reluctant to agree to this because it will produce bad publicity for the library and its lack of security. The curator insists that it is unethical for the library not to report the theft. Reluctantly the director agrees.

The police come and make a report. They say that there is not enough evidence to put the professor under arrest, but that they will question him about the theft. The next day the police call and say that the professor had already checked out of his motel and left town. They can do nothing more. However, they say they will give the library a copy of their report. When it arrives, the report says that lack of security at the library is a contributory cause to the problem. The director is unhappy, but decides he will take action. He will use the report as a basis to ask for additional funding for the library to improve security at the next college budget meeting.

The curator talks the situation over with you because he is still dissatisfied and feels that the professor is the likeliest culprit. You suggest to him that he can use the ArchivesList Web site to post a warning to other institutions to watch the professor if he comes in to do research and to check carefully that nothing goes missing during his visit. You advise him to add a disclaimer that there is no proof that the professor has ever stolen anything, but that your library is missing things from collections he has used.

Case Forty
Karen Benedict, Contributor

You are a project archivist working on a two-year funded grant processing photographs for the Sagamore State College Archives. It is your first job after receiving your master's degree, and you are anxious to do well and make a good impression, as there may be a full-time job available at the end of the grant period when the assistant archivist retires. The staff consists of the archivist, assistant archivist, and a graduate student in addition to you.

You commute from your home, which is located forty-five miles away from the college. You have almost completed your first year on the job. It is summer. One Saturday you go with a friend to your local flea market. You notice the assistant archivist is there and wander over to say hello. He has a table and is selling a variety of things. You look around at what he has for sale and find that among a lot of books, pictures, and postcards are a few old photographs of the Sagamore State College campus, three old yearbooks from the 1940s and 1950s, and pennants and other college memorabilia that look like materials you have in the archives.

You are shocked and can sense that the assistant archivist realizes that you are wondering if these items are college property. He asks you if you want to buy something. When you tell him no, he says he is busy and you had better run along. You stammer a sort of question about how some of the things he has for sale look like things in the archives. He says everything from the college is a duplicate that was being thrown away. He took them from the trash in the same way that most of the stuff for sale here has been scavenged from somewhere.

Is this stolen merchandise?

Will you report what you have seen to the archivist on Monday morning?

If these items actually were thrown into the trash, then the assistant archivist technically did not steal them. However, for him, as an archives employee, to put university items that once were in the archives on sale smacks of impropriety. He is not a thief, but he has not acted professionally in taking these things out of the trash and putting them on sale.

You decide that you will speak with him first on Monday and explain why you think this conduct is wrong. If he agrees to stop raiding the university's trash for his flea market stall, then you don't need to tell the archivist. You can give him the benefit of the doubt and check again later to see if he has stopped this practice. If he says that there is nothing wrong with what he has done, then you should go to the archivist and tell him about your concerns. Because it affects the archives' reputation, he should be aware if this practice continues.

SUGGESTED ADDITIONAL READINGS ON ETHICS

This is not a comprehensive bibliography on the topic of ethics and the archival profession. It is a list of books and articles that will provide the reader with additional information and other perspectives on the subject of professional ethics and its relevancy to the archival profession.

Alderman, Ellen and Caroline Kennedy. *The Right to Privacy*. Vancouver, Wash.: Vintage Books, 1997.

American Library Association, Professional Ethics Committee. "On Professional Ethics (Final Draft of Revised Statement and Code)." *American Libraries* 12 (June 1981): 335.

American Library Association, Professional Ethics Committee. "Statement of Professional Ethics (Final Draft of Revised Statement)." *Arkansas Libraries* 38 (June 1981): 27.

American Library Association, Professional Ethics Committee. "Statement on Professional Ethics (1979 Draft)." *School Library Journal* 26 (November 1979): 14; *American Libraries* 10 (December 1979): 666; *Wilson Library Bulletin* 54 (December 1979): 217.

American Library Association, Special Committee on Code of Ethics. "Statement of Professional Ethics (1975)." *School Library Journal* 26 (November 1979): 14; *American Libraries* 10 (December 1979): 666.

American Library Association, Special Committee on Code of Ethics. "Statement on Professional Ethics, 1975." *American Libraries* 6 (April 1975): 231.

"Aslib and Ethics (Opposing the Application of the Draft Code of Librarians Outside the Public Area)." *Library Association Record* 83 (June 1981): 278.

Barritt, Marjorie. "The Appraisal of Personally Identifiable Student Records." *American Archivist* 49 (Summer 1986): 263–75.

Baumann, Roland M. "The Administration of Access to Confidential Records in State Archives: Common Practices and the Need for a Model Law." *American Archivist* 49 (Fall 1986): 349–69.

Bayles, Michael D. *Professional Ethics*. Belmont, Calif.: Wadsworth Publishing Company, 1981.

Baynes-Cope, A. D. "Ethics and the Conservation of Archival Documents." *Journal of the Society of Archivists* 9, no. 4 (October 1988): 185–87.

Bearman, Toni Carbo. "Do We Need a Code of Ethics for Information Science?" *ASIS Bulletin* 8 (October 1981): 36.

Becker, Ronald L. "The Ethics of Providing Access." *Provenance* 11, nos. 1 & 2 (1993): 57–77.

Benedict, Karen. "Archival Ethics." In *Managing Archives and Archival Institutions*, edited by James Gregory Bradsher. London: Mansell Publishing, 1988.

Bennett, Colin J. *Regulating Privacy, Data Protection and Public Policy in Europe and the United States*. Ithaca, N.Y.: Cornell University Press, 1992.

Boyd, Willard D. "Museum Accountability: Laws, Rules, Ethics and Accreditation." *Curator* 34 (1991): 65–77.

Bradsher, James Gregory. "Privacy Act Expungements: A Reconsideration." *Provenance* 6 (Spring 1988): 1–25.

_____. "We Have a Right to Privacy." In *Constitutional Issues and Archives*. Mid-Atlantic Regional Archives Conference, 1988.

Brascom, Anne W. *Who Owns Information? From Privacy to Public Access*. New York: Basic Books, 1994.

Brichford, Maynard. Introduction to *Provenance* Volume on Ethics. *Provenance* 11, nos. 1 & 2 (1993): 21–24.

Brin, David. *The Transparent Society: Will Technology Force Us to Choose Between Privacy and Freedom?* Boulder, Colo.: Perseus Books, 1999.

Cain, Virginia J. H. "The Ethics of Processing." *Provenance* 11, nos. 1 & 2 (1993): 39–55.

Callahan, Joan C., ed. *Ethical Issues in Professional Life*. New York: Oxford Press, 1988.

Chalou, George. "We Have a Right to Know." In *Constitutional Issues and Archives*. Mid-Atlantic Regional Archives Conference, 1988.

Churchill, Larry R. "The Teaching of Ethics and Moral Values in Teaching." *Journal of Higher Education, Special Issue on Ethics and the Academic Profession* 3 (3) (May–June 1982): 296–306.

Cooke, Anne. "A Code of Ethics for Archivists: Some Points for Discussion." *Archives and Manuscripts* 15 (November 1987): 95–104.

Coyle, Karen. *Coyle's Information Highway Handbook*. Chicago: American Library Association, 1997.

Danielson, Elena. "The Ethics of Access." *American Archivist* 52 (Winter 1989): 52–62.

_____. "Ethics and Reference Services." In *Reference Services for Archives and Manuscripts*, edited by Laura B. Cohen. New York: The Haworth Press, 1997.

Duniway, David. "Conflicts in Collecting." *American Archivist* 24 (January 1961): 55–63.

Duranti, Luciana. "Enforcing the SAA Code of Ethics." *Archival Outlook* (July 1993): 7.

Elston, Charles G. "University Student Records: Research Use, Private Rights and the Buckley Law." *Midwestern Archivist* 1 (1976): 16–32.

Flaherty, David H. "Privacy and Confidentiality: The Responsibilities of Historians." *Reviews in American History* (September 1980): 419–29.

Geselbracht, Raymond H. "The Origins of Restrictions on Access to Personal Papers at the Library of Congress and the National Archives." *American Archivist* 49 (Spring 1986): 142–62.

Goldstein, Bruce D. "Confidentiality and Dissemination of Personal Information, An Examination of State Laws Governing Data Protection." *Emory Law Journal* 41, no. 4 (Fall 1992): 1185.

Hamby, Alonzo L. and Edward Weldon, eds. *Access to the Papers of Recent Public Figures: The New Harmony Conference.* Bloomington, Ind.: Organization of American Historians, 1977.

Hauptman, Robert. "Ethical Commitment and the Professions." *Catholic Library World* 51 (5) (December 1979): 196–99.

"Professionalism or Culpability? An Experiment in Ethics." *Wilson Library Bulletin* 50 (8) (April 1976): 626–27.

Hendricks, Evan, Trudy Hayden, and Jack D. Novick. *Your Right to Privacy: A Guide to Legal Rights in an Information Society.* 2d ed. New York: ACLU, 1990.

Hisson, Richard T. *Privacy in a Public Society: Human Rights in Conflict.* New York: Oxford University Press, 1987.

Hobbs, Bonnie. "Lawyers' Papers: Confidentiality versus the Claims of History." *Washington and Lee Law Review* 49 (Winter 1992): 179–211.

Hodson, Sara S. "Private Lives: Confidentiality in Manuscript Collections." *Rare Books and Manuscript Librarianship* 6 (1991): 108–118.

Hoff-Wilson, Joan. "Access to Restricted Collections: The Responsibility of Professional Historical Organizations." *American Archivist* 46 (Fall 1983): 441–47.

Horn, David. "The Development of Ethics in Archival Practice." *American Archivist* 52 (Winter 1989): 64–71.

Johnson, Oliver A. *Ethics: A Source Book.* New York: Holt, Rinehart and Winston, 1958.

Kahn, Herman. "The Long-Range Implications for the Historians and Archivists of the Charges Against the Franklin D. Roosevelt Library." *American Archivist* 34 (July 1971): 265–75.

Katz, Bill and Ruth A. Fraley, eds. *Ethics and Reference Services*. The Reference Librarian Series Number 4, New York: The Haworth Press, 1982.

Ketelaar, Eric. "Archives of the People, By the People, For the People." In *The Archival Image: Collected Essays*, by Eric Ketelaar. Amsterdam: Hilversum Verloren, 1997.

———. "The Right to Know, the Right to Forget? Personal Information in Public Archives." In *The Archival Image: Collected Essays*, by Eric Ketelaar. Amsterdam: HilversumVerloren, 1997.

Kultgen, John, *Ethics and Professionalism*. Philadelphia: University of Pennsylvania Press, 1988.

———. "Evaluating Codes of Professional Ethics." In *Profits and professions: Essays in Business and Professional Ethics*, edited by Wade L. Robinson, Michael S. Pritchard, and Joseph Ellin. Clifton, N.J.: Humana Press, 1983.

Lankford, Nancy. "Ethics and the Reference Archivist." *Midwestern Archivist* 8 (1983): 7–13.

Lilburn, Rachel. "The NZSA Code of Ethics: Does it Work?" *New Zealand Archivist* 7 (Spring 1996): 8–10.

Lindsey, Jonathan A. and Ann E. Prentice. *Professional Ethics and Librarians*. Phoenix, Ariz.: Oryx Press, 1985.

MacDonald, Robert R. "Developing A Code of Ethics for Museums." *Curator* 34 (1991): 176–86.

MacIntyre, Alasdair. *A Short History of Ethics*. New York: Macmillan, 1973.

MacNeil, Heather. "Defining the Limits of Freedom of Enquiry: The Ethics of Disclosing Personal Information Held in Government Archives." *Archivaria* 32 (Summer 1991): 143–44.

———.*Without Consent: The Ethics of Disclosing Personal Information in Public Archives*. Metuchen, N.J.: Scarecrow Press, 1992.

Mason, Richard O., Florence M. Mason and Mary J. Culnan. *Ethics of Information Management*. Thousand Oaks, Calif.: Sage Publications, 1995.

May, Trevor Ian. "Archival Professionalism and Ethics: An Assessment of Archival Codes in North America." Master of Archival Studies thesis, University of British Columbia, 1995.

Miller, Harold L. "Will Access Restrictions Hold Up in Court: The FBI's Attempt to Use the Braden Papers at the State Historical Society of Wisconsin." *American Archivist* 52 (Spring 1989): 180–90.

Newhall, Anne Clifford. "Access to Archives and Privacy: The Twenty-third International Archival Round Table Conference Proceedings." *American Archivist* 52 (Winter 1989): 64–71.

"Our Ethical Duty in a Free, Civilized Society (Draft Code for Professional Ethics)." *Library Association Record* 83 (August 1981): 367.

Peterson, Kenneth G. "Ethics in Academic Librarianship: The Need for Values." *The Journal of Academic Librarianship* 9 (July 1983): 132–37.

Pemberton, J. Michael and Lee O. Pendergraft. "Toward a Code of Ethics: Social Relevance and the Professionalization of Records Management." *Records Management Quarterly* 24 (April 1990): 3–11.

Polenberg, Richard. "The Roosevelt Library Case: A Review Article." *American Archivist* 34 (July 1971): 277–84.

Rhoads, James B. "Alienation and Thievery: Archival Problems." *American Archivist* 29 (April 1966): 197–208.

Robbin, Alice. "State Archives and Issues of Personal Privacy: Policies and Practices." *American Archivist* 49 (Spring 1986): 163–75.

Russell, E. W. "Archival Ethics." *Archives and Manuscripts* 6 (February 1976): 226–34.

Sellars, Wilfrid and John Hospers. *Readings in Ethical Theory.* 2nd ed. New York: Appleton, Century-Crofts, 1970.

Shopper, Moisy. "Breaching Confidentiality." *Society, Social Science and Modern Society* 29, no. 2 (January/February 1992):24.

Simmons, Ruth. "The Public's Right to Know and the Individual's Right to Be Private." *Provenance* 1 (Spring 1983): 1–4.

Stoddart, Mark. "A Code of Ethics for Archivists." *New Zealand Archivist* 1 (Spring 1990): 8–11.

Stone, Gerald L. "Knowledge and Beliefs about Confidentiality on a University Campus." *Journal of College Student Development* 31, no. 5 (September 1990): 437.

Stewart, Virginia R. "Problems of Confidentiality in the Administration of Personal Case Records." *American Archivist* 37 (July 1974): 387–98.

Sweeney, Shelley. "ACA Ethics Committee." *ACA Bulletin* 15 (May 1991): 1.

White, Louis P. and Kevin C. Wooten. *Professional Ethics and Practice in Organizational Development: A Systematic Analysis of Issues, Alternatives, and Approaches.* New York: Praeger, 1986.

Whyte, Doug. "The Acquisition of Lawyer's Private Papers." *Archivaria* 18 (Summer 1984): 142–53.

Wilsted, Thomas. "Observations on the Ethics of Collecting Archives and Manuscripts." *Provenance* 11, nos. 1 & 2 (1993): 25–37.

Yoxall, Helen. "Privacy and Personal Papers." *Archives and Manuscripts* 12, no. 1 (May 1984): 40.

APPENDIX

Society of American Archivists
CODE OF ETHICS FOR ARCHIVISTS
Revised Version, 1992

The code is a summary of guidelines in the principal areas of professional conduct. A longer commentary explains the reasons for some of the statements and provides a basis for discussion of the points raised.

I. The Purpose of a Code of Ethics

The Society of American Archivists recognizes that ethical decisions are made by individuals, professionals, institutions, and societies. Some of the greatest ethical problems in modern life arise from conflicts between personal codes based on moral teachings, professional practices, regulations based on employment status, institutional policies, and state and federal laws. In adopting a formal code of professional ethics for the Society, we are dealing with only one aspect of the archivist's ethical involvement.

Codes of ethics in all professions have several purposes in common, including a statement of concern with the most serious problems of professional conduct, the resolution of problems arising from conflicts of interest, and the guarantee that the special expertise of the members of a profession will be used in the public interest.

The archival profession needs a code of ethics for several reasons: (1) to inform new members of the profession of the high standards of conduct in the most sensitive areas of archival work; (2) to remind experienced archivists of their responsibilities, challenging them to maintain high standards of conduct in their own work and to promulgate those standards to others; and (3) to educate people who have some contact with archives, such as donors of material, dealers, researchers, and administrators, about the work of archivists and to encourage them to expect high standards.

A code of ethics implies moral and legal responsibilities. It presumes that archivists obey the laws and are especially familiar with the laws that affect their special areas of knowledge; it also presumes that they act in accord with sound moral principles. In addition to the moral and legal responsibilities of archivists, there are special professional concerns, and it is the purpose of a code of ethics to state those concerns and give some guidelines for archivists. The code identifies areas where there are or may be conflicts of interest, and indicates ways in which these conflicting interests may be balanced; the code urges the highest standards of professional conduct and excellence of work in every area of archives administration.

This code is compiled for archivists, individually and collectively. Institutional policies should assist archivists in their efforts to conduct themselves according to this code; indeed, institutions, with the assistance of their archivists, should deliberately adopt policies that comply with the principles of the code.

II. Introduction to the Code

Archivists select, preserve, and make available documentary material of long-term value to the organization or public that the archivist serves. Archivists perform their responsibilities in accordance with statutory authorization or institutional policy. They subscribe to a code of ethics based on sound archival principles and promote institutional and professional observance of these ethical and archival standards.

Commentary: The introduction states the principal functions of archivists: because the code speaks to people in a variety of fields—archivists, curators of manuscripts, records managers—the reader should be aware that not every statement in the code will be pertinent to every worker. Because the code intends to inform and protect non-archivists, an explanation of the basic role of archivists is necessary. The term "documentary materials of long-term value" is intended to cover archival records and papers without regard to the physical format in which they are recorded.

III. Collecting Policies

Archivists arrange transfers of records and acquire documentary materials of long-term value in accordance with their institutions' purposes, stated policies, and resources. They do not compete for acquisitions when competition would endanger the integrity or safety of documentary materials of long-term value, or solicit the records of an institution that has an established archives. They cooperate to ensure the preservation of materials in repositories where they will be adequately processed and effectively utilized.

Commentary: Among archivists generally there seems to be agreement that one of the most difficult areas is that of policies of collection and the resultant practices. Transfers and acquisitions should be made in accordance with a written policy statement, supported by adequate resources and consistent with the mission of the archives. Because personal papers document the whole career of a person, archivists encourage donors to deposit the entire body of materials in a single archival institution. This section of the code calls for cooperation rather than wasteful competition, as an important element in the solution of this kind of problem.

Institutions are independent and there will always be room for legitimate competition. However, if a donor offers materials that are not within the scope of the collecting policies of an institution, the archivist should tell the donor of a more appropriate institution. When two or more institutions are competing for materials that are appropriate for any one of their collections, the archivists must not unjustly disparage the facilities or intentions of others. As stated later, legitimate complaints about an institution or an archivist may be made through proper channels, but giving false information to potential donors or in any way casting aspersions on other institutions or other archivists is unprofessional conduct.

It is sometimes hard to determine whether competition is wasteful. Because owners are free to offer collections to several institutions, there will always be duplication of effort. This kind of competition is unavoidable. Archivists cannot always avoid the increased labor and expense of such transactions.

IV. Relations with Donors, and Restrictions

Archivists negotiating with transferring officials or owners of documentary materials of long-term value seek fair decisions based on full consideration of authority to transfer, donate, or sell; financial arrangements and benefits; copyright; plans for processing; and conditions of access. Archivists discourage unreasonable restrictions on access or use, but may accept as a condition of acquisition clearly stated restrictions of limited duration and may occasionally suggest such restrictions to protect privacy. Archivists observe faithfully all agreements made at the time of transfer.

Commentary: Many potential donors are not familiar with archival practices and do not have even a general knowledge of copyright, provision of access, tax laws, and other factors that affect the donation and use of archival materials. Archivists have the responsibility for being informed on these matters and passing all pertinent and helpful information to potential donors. Archivists usually discourage donors from imposing conditions on gifts or restricting access to collections, but they are aware of sensitive materials and do, when necessary, recommend that donors make provision for protecting the privacy and other rights of the donors themselves, their families, their correspondents, and associates.

In accordance with regulations of the Internal Revenue Service and the guidelines accepted by the Association of College and Research Libraries, archivists should not appraise, for tax purposes, donations to their own institutions. Some archivists are qualified appraisers and may appraise records given to other institutions.

It is especially important that archivists be aware of provisions of the copyright act and that they inform potential donors of any provision pertinent to the anticipated gift.

Archivists should be aware of problems of ownership and should not accept gifts without being certain that the donors have the right to make the transfer of ownership.

Archivists realize that there are many projects, especially for editing and publication, that seem to require reservation for exclusive use. Archivists should discourage this practice. When it is not possible to avoid it entirely, archivists should try to limit such restrictions; there should be a definite expiration date, and other users should be given access to the materials as they are prepared for publication. This can be done without encouraging other publication projects that might not conform to the standards for historical editing.

V. Description

Archivists establish intellectual control over their holdings by describing them in finding aids and guides to facilitate internal controls and access by users of the archives.

Commentary: Description is a primary responsibility and the appropriate level of intellectual control should be established over all archival holdings. A general description inventory should be prepared when the records are accessioned. Detailed processing can be time-consuming and should be completed according to a priority based on the significance of the material, user demand, and the availability of staff time. It is not sufficient for archivists to hold and preserve materials: they also facilitate the use of their collections and make them known. Finding aids, repository guides, and reports in the appropriate publications permit and encourage users in the institution and outside researchers.

VI. Appraisal, Protection, and Arrangement

Archivists appraise documentary materials of long-term value with impartial judgment based on thorough knowledge of their institution's administrative requirements or acquisition policies. They maintain and protect the arrangement of documents and information transferred to their custody to protect its authenticity. Archivists protect the integrity of documentary materials of long-term value in their custody, guarding them against defacement, alteration, theft, and physical damage, and ensure that their evidentiary value is not impaired in the archival work of arrangement, description, preservation, and use. They cooperate with other archivists and law enforcement agencies in the apprehension and prosecution of thieves.

Commentary: Archivists obtain material for use and must ensure that their collections are carefully preserved and therefore available. They are concerned not only with the physical preservation of materials but even more with the retention of the information in the collections. Excessive delay in processing materials and making them available for use would cast doubt on the wisdom of the decision of a certain institution to acquire materials, though it sometimes happens that materials are acquired with the expectation that there would soon be resources for processing them. Some archival institutions are required by law to accept materials even when they do not have the resources to process those materials or store them properly. In such cases archivists must exercise their judgment as to the best use of scarce resources, while seeking changes in acquisition policies or increases in support that will enable them to perform their professional duties according to accepted standards.

VII. Privacy and Restricted Information

Archivists respect the privacy of individuals who created, or are the subjects of, documentary materials of long-term value, especially those who had no voice in the disposition of the materials. They neither reveal nor profit from information gained through work with restricted holdings.

Commentary: In the ordinary course of work, archivists encounter sensitive materials and have access to restricted information. In accordance with their institutions' policies, they should not reveal this restricted information, they should not give any researchers special access to it, and they should not use specifically restricted information in their own research. Subject to applicable laws and regulations, they weigh the need for openness and the need to restrict privacy rights to determine whether release of records or information from records would constitute an invasion of privacy.

VIII. Use and Restrictions

Archivists answer courteously and with a spirit of helpfulness all reasonable inquiries about their holdings, and encourage use of them to the greatest extent compatible with institutional policies, preservation of holdings, legal considerations, individual rights, donor agreements, and judicious use of archival resources. They explain pertinent restrictions to potential users, and apply them equitably.

Commentary: Archival materials should be made available for use (whether administrative or research) as soon as possible. To facilitate such use, archivists should discourage the imposition of restrictions by donors.

Once conditions of use have been established, archivists should see that all researchers are informed of the materials that are available, and are treated fairly. If some materials are reserved temporarily for use in a special project, other researchers should be informed of these special conditions.

IX. Information about Researchers

Archivists endeavor to inform users of parallel research by others using the same materials, and, if the individuals concerned agree, supply each name to the other party.

Commentary: Archivists make materials available for research because they want the information on their holdings to be known as much as possible. Information about parallel research interests may enable researchers to conduct their investigations more effectively. Such information should consist of the previous researcher's name and address and general research topic, and be provided in accordance with institutional policy and applicable laws. Where there is any question, the consent of the previous researcher should be obtained. Archivists do not reveal the details of one researcher's work to others or prevent a researcher from using the same materials that others have used. Archivists are also sensitive to the needs of confidential research, such as research in support of litigation, and in such cases do not approach the user regarding parallel research.

X. Research by Archivists

As members of a community of scholars, archivists may engage in research, publication, and review of the writings of other scholars. If archivists use their institutions' holdings for personal research and publication, such practices should be approved by their employers and made known to others using the same

holdings. **Archivists who buy and sell manuscripts personally should not compete for acquisitions with their own repositories, should inform their employers of their collecting activities, and should preserve complete records of personal acquisitions and sales.**

Commentary: If archivists do research in their own institutions, there are possibilities of serious conflicts of interest—an archivist might be reluctant to show to other researchers material from which he or she hopes to write something for publication. On the other hand, the archivist might be the person best qualified to research in an area represented in institutional holdings. The best way to resolve these conflicts is to clarify and publicize the role of the archivist as researcher.

At the time of their employment, or before undertaking research, archivists should have a clear understanding with their supervisors about the right to research and publish. The fact that archivists are doing research in their institutional archives should be made known to patrons, and archivists should not reserve materials for their own use. Because it increases their familiarity with their own collections, this kind of research should make it possible for archivists to be more helpful to other researchers. Archivists are not obliged, any more than other researchers are, to reveal the details of their work or the fruits of their research. The agreement reached with the employers should include in each instance a statement as to whether the archivists may or may not receive payment for research done as part of the duties of their positions.

XI. Complaints about Other Institutions

Archivists avoid irresponsible criticism of other archivists or institutions and address complaints about professional or ethical conduct to the individual or institution concerned, or to a professional archival organization.

Commentary: Disparagement of other institutions or of other archivists seems to be a problem particularly when two or more institutions are seeking the same materials, but it can also occur in other areas of archival work. Distinctions must be made between defects due to lack of funds, and improper handling of materials resulting from unprofessional conduct.

XII. Professional Activities

Archivists share knowledge and experience with other archivists through professional associations and cooperative activities and assist the professional growth of others with less training or experience. They are obligated by professional ethics to keep informed about standards of good practice and to follow the highest level possible in the administration of their institutions and collections. They have a professional responsibility to recognize the need for cooperative efforts and support the development and dissemination of professional standards and practices.

Commentary: Archivists may choose to join or not to join local, state, regional, and national professional organizations, but they must be well informed about changes in archival functions and they must have some contact with their colleagues. They should share their expertise by participation in professional meetings and by publishing. By such activities, in the field of archives, in related fields, and in their own special interests, they continue to grow professionally.

XIII. Conclusion

Archivists work for the best interests of their institutions and their profession and endeavor to reconcile any conflicts by encouraging adherence to archival standards and ethics.

Commentary: The code has stated the "best interest" of the archival profession—such as proper use of archives, exchanges of information, and careful use of scarce resources. The final statement urges archivists to pursue these goals. When there are apparent conflicts between such goals and either the policies of some institutions or the practices of some archivists, all interested parties should refer to this code of ethics and the judgment of experienced archivists.

N.B.: Copyright of this document belongs to the Society of American Archivists.